WINDRUSH SONGS

James Berry was was born and brought up in a tiny seaside village in Jamaica. When he was 17, he went to work in America, but hated the way black people were treated there, and returned to Jamaica after four years. In 1948, he made his way to Britain, and took a job working for British Telecom.

One of the first black writers in Britain to achieve wider recognition, Berry rose to prominence in 1981 when he won the National Poetry Competition. He has been at the forefront of championing West Indian/British writing and his role as an educator has had a significant impact in mediating that community's experience to the wider society. His numerous books include two seminal anthologies of Caribbean poetry, *Bluefoot Traveller* (1976) and *News for Babylon* (Chatto, 1984), and six collections of poetry, most recently *Hot Earth Cold Earth* (1995) and *Windrush Songs* (2007) from Bloodaxe.

He has published many several books of poetry and short stories for children (from Hamish Hamilton, Puffin and Walker Books), and won many literary prizes, including the Smarties Prize (1987), the Signal Poetry Award (1989) and a Cholmondeley Award (1991). He was awarded an OBE in 1990, elected a Fellow of Birkbeck College in 2001, and given an Honorary Doctorate by the Open University in 2002. He lives in London.

JAMES BERRY

WINDRUSH SONGS

BLOODAXE BOOKS

ISBN: 978 1 85224 770 6

First published 2007 by
Bloodaxe Books Ltd,
Highgreen,
Tarset,
Northumberland NE48 1RP.

www.bloodaxebooks.com
For further information about Bloodaxe titles
please visit our website or write to
the above address for a catalogue.

Bloodaxe Books Ltd acknowledges
the financial assistance of
Arts Council England, North East.

Cover design: Neil Astley & Pamela Robertson-Pearce.

Cover printing: J. Thomson Colour Printers Ltd, Glasgow.

Printed in Great Britain by
Bell & Bain Limited, Glasgow, Scotland.

To Myra
with love and gratitude
for her support in
developing this book

ACKNOWLEDGEMENTS

Acknowledgements are due to the editors of the following publications, in which some of these poems first appeared: *Ambit* (London) and *Wasifiri* (London).

CONTENTS

INTRODUCTION

In 1948 the SS *Empire Windrush*, an ex-troopship, sailed from the Caribbean to Tilbury Docks and initiated the biggest movement of Caribbean people to Britain. The *Windrush* came at such an important time for me and young men of my generation. To find yourself having left school in Jamaica with no prospect of further education, desperate to develop yourself and without any hope of a job, was devastating. We were left stranded, with an overwhelming sense of waste.

None of us wanted to grow up poverty stricken. We didn't want to grow up without knowledge of the world. We certainly didn't want to grow up like our fathers who were stuck there, with a few hills of yams, a banana field, and a few animals. That could not feed a family, let alone provide money for anything more. We were a generation without advanced education or training, anxious about our future. Some of us had shown great promise at school, but now we were stuck, most of our parents could not pay for our further education and there were no national projects to employ us. And here we were, hating the place we loved, because it was on the verge of choking us to death.

This was the state of the Caribbean at that time. The culture was suffering from its history. It was in a state of helplessness. In fact we had not emerged from slavery; the bonds were still around us. There were no government initiatives to improve the people's situation – the government was ineffectual.

I escaped from this situation for a brief while during the period 1942 to 1946. America had run into a shortage of farm labourers and was recruiting workers from Jamaica to help with farm work during the war. I was eighteen at the time. My friends and I, all anxious for improvement and change, were snapped up for this war work and we felt this to be a tremendous prospect for us. Getting away to America gave me a sense of relief, the possibility of having work and getting money for it gave hope, and there was always the prospect of being able to better ourselves and improve our education.

But we soon realised, as we had been warned, that there was a colour problem in the United States that we were not at all familiar with in the Caribbean. America was not a free place for black people; there were too many restrictions on them. That insulted me as a human being and made me see Americans as a nation of small-minded, self-loving white people.

When I came back from America at the end of my contract, pretty soon the same old desperation of being stuck began to affect me. I really wanted to be educated and I couldn't find a way of doing it. I tried correspondence courses to develop my English; I did a course in mechanical dentistry – which I eventually found I had no possibility of practising. When the *Windrush* came along it was a godsend, but I wasn't able to get on that boat. I simply could not meet the expenses. Apart from the fare, everybody knew that you needed decent clothes and shoes for England, and some money to live on until you got a job. It was some time before I was able to get myself together and sell the few pigs and goats I had to gather up the money. Two of my special friends from school went on the *Windrush* but I had to wait for the second ship to make the journey that year, the SS *Orbita*.

War changed a lot of things. It took people away from their home circumstances; it showed them a wider world. After the war people knew that you could travel and change your life. It had far-reaching consequences.

We were going to England. Despite the aftermath of slavery there was still a respect for England and a sense of belonging. Origins are so important, people need a base of knowing where they come from. We knew that in England you could continue education while you worked, you could go to evening school. But England was also the home of the slave masters, and we retained a general distrust of white men. However, England was the nearest thing we had to a mother country; we saw in it some aspect of hope. Africa was hopeless, there was no expectation that Africa could do anything for us. We felt a tremendous disappointment, even a hatred, for a mother country which could sell our ancestors as slaves.

On the SS *Orbita* we talked about the horror of slavery and how it had happened. We talked about the years of no-pay work our ancestors had done for the English. We talked about our own voyage and how we were going to see the England that we'd read about in our school books, where everything was good and shining and moral. We felt part of the possibility of a new way of life, a democratic way of life, in which we would be equal human beings.

Life on the boat brought people together from different islands – I had never had any contact with people from the other Caribbean islands. It was a time of meeting, to talk about our different customs, our island foods, our stories. We longed to understand that we had a background of culture that we shared and that had a deep meaning for us. We also shared a sense of opportunity and expectation about our journey, we were extending our experience as black people in the world. But there was apprehension and anxiety too about what we would find in Britain, and mock panics about whether the boat would be sent back. There was a deep fear and anxiety about what life would hold for us.

When we arrived in England we were well received. There had been a war and there was a tremendous drive to rebuild the country and clear up the mess, so there was no trouble in finding work. We frequently encountered fairness and humanitarianism among the English (far more than I had encountered in the USA). But we would also encounter racism and prejudice, the difficulty of finding a lodging, the difficulty of being seen as an ordinary decent young man, just because you had a black skin. To be a black person in the British way of life has sometimes been a wearying experience; coping with white people's inward dread of a black face is a daily business.

Writing *Windrush Songs*

Windrush has huge significance for me and my fellow West Indians. I was writing these poems for some years. I meant them to be a reflection of the world I grew up in. Into the book I wanted to put my love of nature and of human nature. I wanted to celebrate Caribbean people, their humour, their hopefulness, their capacity for working and never giving up, their worship of God, their sense of love. I felt compelled to write about them, and especially about my own village people with their Caribbean dialect speech.

That language – the way we've retained something of Africa in our voice, mixed up with English-speaking – is the language I grew up with. And I wanted my poems to be identified with my background roots; it gives me pleasure to use this language in poetry. It is a language with a folk strength that I trace back to Africa. And it is concrete, full of images, a good language for poetry.

I kept writing these poems and they developed slowly over the years. It was a way of going back and retrieving my Caribbean experience while I was living in the UK. It was a way of hearing and preserving Caribbean village voices, of juxtaposing them. I found these characters in myself and I got into them through their voices and through their thinking: their hopes, their frustrations, their sense of themselves in the world. They represent an assessment of the time I grew up in.

The whole background of the book is the Jamaican landscape and its extraordinary wild beauty. It's a personal celebration of the wonder of being. In spite of the negative aspects of the history that my ancestors endured, there is so much that gives me tremendous joy in the land I was born in. I see in its natural loveliness an over-whelming reason for life.

The challenge of change

The difference and variety of our human family more and more seems to me to be a wise provision that has come out of nature. The varied faces of people in the world hold something good for each other, but a lack of development in the human race still wants to deprive some peoples of their full human rights. The bigger meaning of the voyage of the *Windrush* was that it brought change to two peoples: those who had come from a background of slavery in the Caribbean, and those whose society had benefited from that slave labour. Movements of people bring change and opportunities for development and enlightenment. The world before *Windrush* was not civilised and fair enough, too many people were left out and disregarded, despite the great contribution they and their ancestors had made. The coming of these Caribbean people has moved things on and made an impact on British society. Our coming together is a challenge and a hope for all.

PART 1

HATING A PLACE YOU LOVE

Wind-rush

I'd like to set out a storm
watching it like the dream it is
watching the sea come
emptying its folds of boats

Watching towering palmtrees fall
across the backs of running cattle
watching the wind carry trees
and drop them on top of shack roofs

Hearing leaves of branches whistle –
I won't miss how breezeblow madness
batter and beat the place up island-wide
knocking things over with sea raging and raging

How island-wide bugle-blow of wind
batter and mash-up the place

break up big limb and banana leaf – them
in nothing but a day of wind-rush –
screaming
            plundering
                        crying.

Learning Beauty

Growing up beside a pothole road
of dirt and gravel
from early I see
joyful skills in riding a donkey bareback
at a place wide for a cart or, best,
a banana truck to whine through.

My tastes are sharp,
I know the trees where all wild fruits grow.
Often well reddened
or blackened with wild grown berries
my tongue finds joyful things.

Alive at dusk, a sudden blanket of night
in a yard of trees —
bats come swarming for ripe fruit
squeaking like rats.

My ears find joyful sounds
coming from squeals of pigs
jostling for space near mother hog,
coming from cockcrow all around the village,
coming from goats tethered in weeds around the yard.

Where Christmas is out of doors I feel beauty
in bursting of clappers and rockets shooting,
in grilling of barbecue pigs in backyards,
in mixing of homemade sorrel drinks and rum punch.

Watching the joy of embraces
in the thrill of voices
I learn the beauty of tenderness.

Wash of Sunlight

Oh, the sun has washed me,
penetrated my skin, my body,
my ways of open fields, and imprinted me
with the glow of sunrise and sunset.

I marvel at the burst of seeds to sunlight
and the careless giving of water over rocks.

Watching the sun rising
I feel I have more than its force in me.
Like the sun overhead at midday
I feel much greater distances
are here sunken in me.

Watching the moon reflected in water,
held by the awe of water,
held by awesome feelings, I know
much greater and more awesome depths
somewhere inside of me.

I stand on the land. I touch
fire, touch water, feel air.

Sitting up Past Midnight

I used to get up some midnight
and come sit at mi doorway
a-think, a-think, a-smoke mi pipe.

I a-think about mi crops –
about mi fields of yams and bananas,
worryin about breeze-blow-hurricane
breakin up mi yam vines an blowin down
mi full banana bunches, ready fo market.

I a-think about mi donkey
how him is sick and don't get up.
Him just picky picky –
a straw stay in his mouth
and him don't chew it.

I a-think about mi third boy child –
always learnin lessons in lamplight –
readin bright-bright, recitin bible passage-them,
now him need extra teachin for examination
and how, how I gwan pay extra teachin?

Then I get strange feelin, a-think
back on mi ancestors them and slave life.
I realise how much of mi history I can't fill in.

Yet – I wake up to come sit
at mi doorway, thinkin,
thinkin about that dead past of mine

seein how mi life face midnight
widhout one lamplight.

Desertion

Dicko Parks gone from him house
and wife, children, dog, donkey
and the land-piece him jus start planting.

Dicko Parks lef not one clue
to show if him gone up, down
or if him vanish sideways
like when him lef Africa
inside him forefathers them.

Him taxes not paid.
Water come down through him roof.
Him stray donkey taken into pound
cos it ol rope bust up.

Three long months now come and gone.
Dicko Parks lef like him gone to him land –
no nightfall bring him back since.
Him wet-eye wife stop search and inquire.
Him sad sad children still skip and play.

I African They Say

I hear people say I African, yet
I know I never seen one, never hear one
and dohn know who he is at all.

If I talk African, is
no more than water a-babble
or bird a-sing at day-clean.

I hear some people say
I dance like African. Yet, fo me, I do
no more than breeze a ruffle tree top.

Africa a blank in mi head
like slave plantations – gone.
I was always at sea, lost.

My ancestors, unknown or despised,
like strangers who threaten me –
I was always lost, at sea.

Harnessed, overworked, never paid,
like any horse or mule,
ancestors were all at sea.

Africa threw ancestors to wild raging sea –
Africa never gestured care to restore me –
just as Africa sold and abandoned me
I can never consider Africa.

Villagers Talk Frustrations

At sunset men begin to gather
coming from fields, from lands in the hills,
putting down their loads,
sitting on the low concrete terrace
in the village square,
across the road from the rum-bar.

Sitting under the dusky open sky,
light reflecting from the two shops,
glow of sunset quietly vanishing
behind the hill.

Sitting on slabs in the dimlit square –
coconut palm limbs, banana leaves, hibiscus, waving.
Confessions – men in bare-feet and in motor-tyre sandals
talk of no-pay and of storms
that killed their crops, smashed up their shacks
and emptied their pockets.

>   First man:
>   *Contention wid miself*
>   *is when I sell a goat, a pig,*
>   *two or three chicken, to know*
>   *which open mouth to put*
>   *the few shillin in.*

As night sky darkens, village voices increase
around the square. Enlivened with two rums
men talk about their day,
about their crops, about their families.
Sudden jokes break out
in playful hopefulness.

>   Second man:
>   *Man, like lots of odders here*
>   *I walk like I did born barefoot*
>   *all thru mi child days*
>   *till young man days, when*
>   *I a-dream bout fat leg-dem –*
>   *wha wi hol yu an sink yu.*

Crickets chirp around the night voices.
Frogs croak, nightingale sings mysteriously
from high trees. Cows moo for their pent calves,
dogs bark around the village. Children's shouts
echo, playing, before dark comes down.

Across their noise
a woman's voice comes like a sad song:

> Woman:
> *Man, when me look pon time*
> *is no laughy-laughy business –*
> *is a sunhot work and work on*
> *wash-wash wid weepin like sweat.*
> *Man – anywhere, let alone Englan,*
> *Me would a-go anywhere blind.*

Now dim shapes of men, one by one, in small groups,
move into shadows of the road
talking garrulously across each other
in emphatic voices
that die away little by little
as they turn off into own yards.

> Third man:
> *Man – you can't stay static*
> *you can't stay stuck*
> *you can't stay locked up or sunk.*
> *You travel on, noh!*
> *Man – you can't stay fixed, frightened,*
> *hating a place you love.*
> *You travel on, noh!*

Like penned pigs are quiet
tethered goats don't bleat
sharp lights of the square go
and the voices gesture in darkness.

Old Slave Villages

The windmills are dead
Their tombs are empty towers

Where high estate walls are broken down
wire fences control the boundaries

Thatched slave shacks are gone
In their place – zinc houses, gardens

The great houses, now derelict,
turned to school grounds – or hotels

The vast fields of sugar cane
are pastures, with cattle grazing

The tombs of landscape windmills
are broken empty towers.

Poverty Life

Hungry children keep hungry mothers
hungry mothers rear hungry children
and children go to school on nothing.

With land, two mules and a bicycle
a man can dance and get drunk
in the mouldy, sweet musky smell of dirty lives –
held captive by poverty.

Like captive by slavery
captive by poverty is
a continuous memory.

Leave the country for the town
to sit in bare earth backyards
or walk the streets hustling
threatened by rentman, police and rats.

Wear lucky garbage shoes
clothes wash and patch
pick up bottles to sell for bread.
Go home to broken windows
rainstained ceilings and walls.

Not enough of anything except children.
Working children are truanting children
or hustling children
or children listless
in the sticky heat of muddy earth floor.

Poverty Ketch Yu an Hol Yu

A trap ketch yu, naked
an hol yu dere, naked!

Yu ketch up ina poverty trap
Great House get yu fi servant
Great House dog keep yu it servant

Cokanut oil will shine up yu hair
you trousers press sharp sharp –
but pocket dem empty, empty like husk

Then man you throw you trousers –
only throw you trousers on the bed –
few days later, man, she pregnant again!

A morning time take yu
an swing yu like dead puss
then – it pick yu up again
an swing yu like dead puss

Seven day a week man
seven day a week
you a-move like dead puss.

Devouring

Between night and high sun
moistness of early morning has its hunger
snails and slugs search

A rush of leaves rustle
hens flutter up with a terror cackle
devourer mongoose lurks

Cool evening raises desire
with jaw-butchering sounds
mother hog gobbles another piglet

And soon she has dined
on her birth-given nine –
then she'll be fattened to be pieces of meat

Imprisoned in helpless poverty
most of us are lifers – a shame pronounced
when meeting the well-fed and prosperous,
overpowering in their dress, voices, confidence.

Sea-Song One

Come on
Seawash of travel
Expose new layers of skin

Come on calm voice of sea
Come and settle on land

Sea's tumble wash
Change our rags for riches

Come on – tumble wash of sea
Clear away the bloody waters
      Clear away the bloody waters

PART 2

LET THE SEA BE MY ROAD

Reasons for Leaving

Sea-Song Two

Beginner of life –
tossing-place of waves like mountains,
racetrack for wild headlong winds,
world cemetery of bones and wrecks.

Mother with your salt in my veins
waving veils of lace around your body,
your mysteries give me dreams.

Drummer in your sea-bottom caves,
depths with echoes of cathedral sounds.

Let's say you wanted to collect me up –
now frightened and hopeful I go.
Your roads of travel lead on
        to rebirth after rebirth.

Reasons for Leaving Jamaica

Mi one milkin' cow did jus' die!
Gone, gone – an' leave me worthless
like hurricane disaster.

Then, mi neighbour stoned, stoned
and killed mi dog, and I did know
I would move – move well away.

Man, when I did come happy, happy to reap
mi first four bunch of bananas
from mi new half acre of land
and, man, find every one newly cut and gone
I did move about shattered,
dazed in a crazy spin of a dream.

That half acre did take me ten year to buy –
mi little land-piece of bananas was
mi pride an' hope an' sense of achievement.
Now, a man did come and reap mi first crop.
I did know there and then that if I did kill him,
him couldn't come back and come back!

Then, man, I did go tired, tired.
Like miself, mi piece of land
did sit there tired – tired.
Windrush did jus'come an' save me an' him.

Running on Empty

Man, I been running on empty all my life
simply hoping I somehow get there
feeling like I a burnt-out mash-up engine
never recharged, never refuelled.

Yes, man, I was the bullcow with eight legs
moving houses whole,
pulling heavy goods and felled trees,
taking on everybody's load.

I was the mechanical beast,
bulge-eyed, dragging dead weight,
and now it's strange, feeling
this change that might make me man.

I was the rusty worn-out machine
running too much on empty
carrying other people's lives.
Now – legs are trying to walk away.

This travel never happened before.
I was a fixed area of midnight,
my sunburnt face provoked
indifference or just non-recognition.

Man, let me try open new eyes
on mystery of new horizons.
Let me walk beside the scents
of new and unknown petals in bloom.

Let my doings and new recognition
wash emotions clean of gains and losses
cleanse both wealth and poverty of harsh feelings
and even stir nations to look and be widened.

To Travel This Ship

To travel this ship, man
I gladly strip mi name
of a one-cow, two-goat an a boar pig
an sell the land piece mi father lef
to be on this ship and to be a debtor.

Man, jus fa diffrun days
I woulda sell, borrow or thief
jus fa diffrun sunrise an sundown
in annodda place wid odda ways.

To travel this ship, man
I woulda hurt, I woulda cheat or lie,
I strip mi yard, mi friend and cousin-them
To get this yah ship ride.

Man – I woulda sell mi mudda
Jus hopin to buy her back.
Down in dat hole I was
I see this lickle luck, man,
I see this lickle light.

Man, Jamaica is a place
Where generations them start out
Havin notn, earnin notn,
And – dead – leavin notn.

I did wake up every mornin
and find notn change.
Children them shame to go to school barefoot.
Only a penny to buy lunch.

Man, I follow this lickle light for change.
I a-follow it, man!

A Dream of Leavin

Man, so used to notn, this is
a dream I couldn't dream of dreamin,
so – I scare I might wake up.

One day I would be Englan bound!
A travel would have me on sea
not chained down below, every tick of clock,
but free, man! Free like tourist!

Never see *me* coulda touch world of Englan –
when from all accounts I hear
that is where all we prosperity end up.

I was always in a dream of leavin.
My half-finished house was on land
where work-laden ancestors' bones lay.

The old plantation land still stretch-out
        down to the sea,
                giving grazing to cattle.

Breaking Free

Man – is a kind of lockup I grow in
why I had to battle on
with bare hands
to crack walls.

Inside, longings twist me
for money, for songs, for paintings,
for knowledge
of what I should become
out of tracks and lacks.

The meanness of people
with arms lengthened
with greed, with guns, with pens,
that worked with voices clean and cool!

I long and long
to know why
bigness is power to hurt most
and not power for most peace.

Haunted by a harsh business running me
I study how knowledge sharpens weapons,
study living by losses, study how
to show up cruelties.

Powerless, I tremble so stupidly
facing jailer threats.
Yet I know I *must* work on
work on, work on.

All the time searching
into day-start,
I'm reclaiming old wisdom
in new music I make.

Breaking free
        in my world
to see more, feel more, freely wander –
        become more.

Away from Mi Little Ova-bodda Piece of Lan

Away from mi little ova-bodda piece of lan,
mi house of leaves – mi little leaf house.

Mi lame donkey will rest.
Mi maaga dog will wonda
why, why I dohn call him.

None of them will know
I gone in hope, trusting a big hearty God,
to work for proud people who lucky wid money.

Away fram everyday roastin in sun-hot
fram day-by-day sweat wash
an fram no-ice, half-warm water...

To keep me barefoot children in ABC school
I shun all bodderation day dem
to go try workin with proud-proud people
who *lucky*, man, *lucky* wid money.

Land-Cultivator-Man at Sea

Though soil did colour mi finger-them,
birdsong and sunblaze did fill mi head,
an mi easy pace did face no whiphand –
now, I travel like I get carried.

While, evening time, rum did talk
mi non-book talk, in distric rum bar,
I marvel how I couldn jus keep on
and not travel, like now I get carried.

Though terror weekend-them did come
all empty-pocketed, wid a wretched house,
mi family did sleep close an warm –
travellin now, I'm carried into ice.

From what I hear, a man mus give up
someting old for someting new.
Workin a machine wohn be same like
castratin cockerel, ram-kid or bull-calf.

Bein hospital orderly wohn be like
stoppin fever with hot bath
of herbs, barks, and sweet oils, nor
like carin for fields of young bananas.

So let the sea be my road –
S.S. *Windrush* be my carriage –
and human change my hope.

A Woman's Dread of Layered Snow

Layered snow stirs my terror.
Generations of snow frighten me:
their ice has brushed me.

I dread hearts of no-sunshine
and bleak inherited snow faces.
Yet, I got fixed up to stow away.

My sister rescued me. She dug
deep and loaned me cash
for my full passage money.

Twenty five years old, three children.
No father help. No job. And back
in country home, with parents.

I had started to train as nurse –
then first child happened.
Now I want back my nursing:

I want opportunity to be myself
becoming who I know I am –
I want university for all my children.

I don't want to lose cockcrowing
of my parents' yard,
or the coming coming waves of their seaside.

But I don't want desires and distractions.
I want peace, time to qualify. Even a lockup
like a strict convent would suit me.

Man, me did have too much sunshine.
Now me want some snowtime.
Me could do with a place sun-forgotten –

That's why I happily go
where half the year nothing grow.
Man – let's build praises for snow.

Work Control Me Fadda Like a Mule

Work control me fadda like a mule,
control me modda like a jackass,
yet, stubborn stubborn,
life pass we
an *that* we full house live on.

Circle of hard time suck out we place
hold we like bad obeah spell
have we like skeletons –
starvation beget we.

Hungriness develop me
like rock a-want wings-them
but sunshine flood me,
and roast me and dry me inside.

But, rain bring hope
and wet me tongue and toes-them,
Rain-storm drench me
and sea-water wash me.

And now, sea a-carry me
headlong to a little change –
and here me a-shake
with hopefulness
            about what I goin *do* with it.

Sea-Song Three

Earth's twin sister – old sea –
carry me on your mother back
above unsteady bones, whitening whiter

Like wishes and dreams, complete cities
are transient skylines, sometimes looking
lit up with hanging stars

Life moves on your surface
like meteor that crashed
into a moment and shattered it

I want to feel safe like a sitting gull
on your back, dreaming of fishing places

Facing sky, let me lie
on you, swaying,
reading each star's biography

Let me ride with you to your shores'
four corners, finding balance of blends
in looks, thoughts, voices.

Reminiscence Voices

Reminiscence Voice

Man, I want to go back to hear
hilltop cockcrow giving
answer to bottom yard rooster challenge
mother cow giving anxious 'moo'
for a calf keeping cool in the shade –
     I want to renew all that.

Man, I want to go back to hear
cooing of ground-doves in quiet noon-time
and tree-top nightingales singing
to the moon long before daylight –
     I want to renew all that.

Man, I want to go back to have
a curry-goat feed under coconut palms
rum flowing like a nature stream
and conchshell blowing for a big sea catch –
     I want to renew all that.

Man, I want to go back to hear
Maama Tunny passing to church
fanning herself, calling
     'Good-morning' to our house.

The Rock

Me not goin back to dat hell Jamaica.
Me have more pain there than I can tell.
Sun-hot burn me up outside –
rain wahn drown me inside mi house.

Me dohn go back to no damn Jamaica
wha all-a-we call – 'The Rock'.
Rocky road burst up me toe-dem.
Hungry belly wahn me walk like skeleton.

Me not gohn back Jamaica.
Only white-man-dem –
users of mi mind an body –
call Jamaica paradise:
not me, made from sweat an curse.

I leavin the Rock.
I dohn intend to go back.
Only outside people-dem call Jamaica 'beautiful'.

So-so breadfruit not gohn force me to eat it.
Dry time not gohn have me shrivel-up.
Satday night not gohn find me an empty pocket
listenin foolishness in-a rum-bar.

No sar – early cockcrow fa wake-up
not gohn drag me outa bed to starve me.
Monday to Monday gohn find me – absent!
Mi jackass no-pay force me to move.

Me not gohn back Jamaica.
Only poverty there mould a man.
Only touris-dem see it paradise.
No sar! That sea sound not gohn reach me.
Ground dove cooin not gohn fill-up mi ears.

Thinkin of Joysie

When I think of Joysie, man,
I goin wahn fly back instantly –
but, Joysie dohn like hurry-hurry
even though she the rudest village girl.

Joysie is a winna, all sweeta,
she give you what she have
like she is belly of the movin sea
but, calm, she jus like an early dusk
afta sleep satisfy you good, good.

Joysie can cry out like you kill her
when you hear her cry out, saying:
You, you, you think you is Jesus
opening Paradise door!
And so wiry, you cahn believe how she move.

Joysie has the bigges heart,
the stronges body, most cutting scream.
She takes you like a tidal wave
takes a canoe, leavin sea, sky
an jus one little bird.

Man, Joysie have hot temper
but her big big givin is cool.
Joysie make sure you cahn forget her.
Joysie has no keep-quiet manners –
half the village men *love* Joysie.

Mi Woman Hol Everyting Back

Mi woman hol
everyting back –
everyting back

Even in bed she wahn hide –
she wrap up sheself –
nevva make a firs move

Mi woman hol
everyting back, you know,
she hol everyting back

Even – our baby did take
a hell of a pulling out
to get her to let it go

Mi woman hol
everyting back –
everyting back

She don cry yu know –
even when I hol her to kiss goodbye
I get the back of her neck

But I still dohn wahn her
hol everyting back every day, every day,
widout me bein there

Man – me cahn stay long a Englan.

Fish Talk

Talk about mi oily-mout dish –
then talk only fish.

Fried fish, stewed fish, creole and escovitch fish
or jus red snapper in papillote

Man – notn make me forget
great crab-back flake

Or creamed lobster with butter and
stamp-and-go saltfish frittas

Give me plateful of little sprats fried up
an spiced with pepper, salt, pimento grains

Man I sweat – gone in the mood
jus talkin nice peppery food.

Sun-Hot Drink

1

Jelly-coconut water –
from baby coconut growing –
full of water inside.
Drunk in the field, man, in sun-hot:
break coconut's thick husk with machete
and, sweating, open it –
find the inside white river
find coolness, man, fruitiness,
that soft sweet taste
from sun, tree, air.

2

Sunlight's dominion claims
water, water, man, water:
you get one drink
and you're gone, man
down stream
like a log afloat wallowing off
all sweat. And you move
again. Move again, man.

3

White rum, white rum: man
that's fabric of sun caught
to be reborn inside of you
and have you laced from head
to toe, burning, man, sweet, sweet!

Empire Day

Empire Day is what me rememba, singin
praises to Modder Country, Englan.
At home, me put on mi church shoes
an mi new likkle khaki trousers an shirt
an meet other spruced-up distric
children-them. Stiffly, happily on we go.

At school, we have prayers. We recite
poems about Englan and Empire. Each
one of us get a likkle Union Jack
and sweets with flags printed
all over the tin.

Other schools join we. And, drilled,
marchin around the schoolyard, aroun
our wide and high, high poinciana tree
covered wid red flowers, our likkle
Union Jack them a-wave and a-flutta.
We sing we heart out, singing 'Rule
Britannia', glowin with all we loyal
virtue to King, Country and Empire.

In jollification, we play games.
We eat jerk pork, fresh bread, candy
an spicy cake. We eat snowball an drink
cool drinks. Mi Union Jack sweets-tin
turn mi treasure, keeping
mi slate pencil an mi marble-them.

Childhood Mysteries

We believed we knew what parents knew.
We knew what children could not make
they could not have. We could not make shoes –
only goodluck children wore shoes to school.
Our feet on school floor were mostly feet
we ourselves dressed with a wash.

We ourselves made our wheels and kites,
made our balls and bats. We looked always
to find a nail, a piece of crate-wood
and a good piece of string. But
we collected up a mango season
or starapple season in our laps,
in our pockets, in our bags.

Innocent of history happenings,
we played like goat-kids
around the tower of the stilled windmill,
between the crumbling wall stumps
of the old slave estate sugar mill –
we ran about on the iron uprights, half buried.

Busy with our children's aimless work,
unconscious of the site of old slave huts,
we found glass pieces in our yard
and pieces of clay jars, bowls and pots
like treasures for their colours and shapes.
Scared to touch them, mystified, and perhaps
dreading unclean contact,
not speaking, we dropped the pieces
for the earth to swallow again.

Tramping on about our endless business
unaware of the burial grounds of slaves
we tumbled on graves in the woods
or in a coconut walk. Quickly
we made the sign of the cross
and noted to avoid the spot.

In adulthood gradually
we connected these pieces together
and kept on coming on, making maps of time.

Old Slave Plantation Village Owner

She lived alone with many dogs:
the rich white queen of our village.
My father and my brother worked for her.
I worked as her teenage butler and
nursed her pet bulldog, that she worshipped.

Nearly all the village ancestors
had laboured for her ancestors
as house slaves, field slaves,
sugar plantation slaves:
she was respected as a royal person.

Her modern fenced-off house with broad verandahs,
built on foundations of the Old Great House,
was near the ruins of the sugar mill
on raised ground, with gardens.
Her lands were like an ocean around her.

She inherited no culture, nor developed any,
of assisting slave descendants
with education, health, or advancement.
She entertained the rich
in celebrations, under electric stars.
Everything in her house was shining.

She would not assist my further education –
yet she would sit me down
in a cushioned fall-back chair
and play her piano to me,
using me as audience.

And first European music
to impress me deeply, played
on His Master's Voice gramophone,
was her favourite record and love song:
John McCormack's tenor voice
singing 'Yours is my heart alone'.

A boy cannot caress
a grand lady's isolated heart:
he is less than her dogs.
He takes her outrages and curses
on serving her food and cleaning her rum glasses,
her shoes, her ashtrays.
In moonlight, between shaven hedges
of jasmine, among whitewashed palm tree trunks,
he serves answers to questions
about village gossip.

I heard the nightingale
and never mentioned it.
You were a crystal voice, perfumed.
I gave you honour for your wealth –
        created by whip and gun.

Comparing Now with Ancestors' Travel from Africa

The first time when ancesta-them did travel
them did a-travel to lose tongue, name
and pay. This time, descendant-them
a-travel by choice, with hope, and with
resolution for fulfilment.

The first time when ancesta-them did travel
them did a-travel pile up in a ship hole,
chained-up, angry, filthy, half starved.
This time descendant-them a-travel free
a-si moonlight on big sea.

The first time when ancesta-them did travel
them did a-travel to reach shore bruise up, half dead.
Some leave them bones a-push about by big sea.
This time, descendant-them a-travel
to reach in-a clean Sunday clothes.

The first time when ancesta-them did travel
them did a-travel in-a dread bout
where they would reach, and specially
would they reach as meat on white-man table.

This time, descendant-them, head full of hope,
droppin off all the past – a-look forward
to a-share skills, wealth and recognition –
determined to be humanly respected.

And some may yet a-travel
to write down them ancesta story.

A Talk to the Machete

A slow-speaking man said:
If, goin, I close a history chapta
of time ancesta-them did have machete
slap in them hand – and that does mean
I drop you fi good – machete,
I will be glad I said goodbye.

If I lose you – my beatin-time stick, given me
to sweetn the world with sugar and money,
widdout pay or pension to me, and, when I rest,
to be the silva snake beside me –
machete, I will be glad I said goodbye.

If I leave you forever – my heavy, busy
pen, that mark acres, keep me sweatin
but bring no pay – and *maybe* one day
even should draw on that ol-time account,
machete, I will be glad I said goodbye.

If my daily slave-maker – who often
did stay in tree-shady with me and my dog,
and at night stay leaned up indoors
like a beatin-stick – you should gone
dead, like somebody cold and stiff,
machete, I will be glad I said goodbye.

If – my overgripped handle, my steel blade
companion, my careless wounder,
who chop your way through centuries
to make me African-Jamaican-British –
I should go beyond you into new chapta,
machete, you done your last job. Now – goodbye.

A Story I Am In

They thought we were lost, wandering
more than they were.
Their leader pulled his gun and wounded
one of us, we tried to help our wounded.
They tied us to walk with their wagons.

We became lost in time.
The days buzzed their arrivals
and their worn paths of departures:
no saviour in the world.

And like trees' absorption of sun change
at work, our flame sometimes ignited
bright flashes, while mostly
smouldering, fading, dying little by little.

We were drilled to know that
our tongues moved like leaden frogs,
our hands were blunt machetes,
our milkers reported we gave dirt
and ashes.

And waiting on slow time
we sang sadly in chains
not seeing the gold our hands wove.

They staged us showing how well
we splintered stones with our hands,
carried a mule on our backs,
ate rags, wood shavings and shit.

They talked like clanging metal,
fought like bulls clashing heads,
using voices like sea sounds in caves.

Devoured, our time was their sweetness of meat
and their energy of power.
Every day sunrises herded us
into fields that ground us like mills.

And our blood premium – Sugar –
hoisted the flags of kings
and made their horns of power music.

Mi Fight with Jack-Jack

I wonda, always wonda, if
mi fight with Jack-Jack didn kill him.

Satday evening, everybody at village square –
Jack-Jack an me there – fo death.

Since we fight, Jack-Jack never is
that man him was like before.

Since we fight, him head droop
an him nevva walk straight again.

Jack-Jack walk with a hold-up
Like sometn did cut – up in him hip.

Jack-Jack did hit me to kill me.
Him give me pain I neva, neva did feel.

Jack-Jack did pick me up, lick me down
and jump up-and-down in-a mi face.

Him did fight me to kill me dead –
I did fight him with *all* mi vengeance.

Mi head, mi hand, mi heart, all
did hit him, hurt him, overpower him.

If Jack-Jack did have him machete
him woulda chop me up –

him woulda lash me up all over
with straight straight streak of blood.

Him did fight me to kill me dead –
I did fight him to stay on mi foot.

I believe – I know – we fight did kill him.
Him did suffer fram it bad.

We fight did slow-slow make him sink
and in time go rotten-rotten.

When I go to Englan now
I goin sen him wife some money,

I goin sen Jack-Jack wife money.
I goin sen him wife some money – regular.

Sea-Song Four

Reflecting endlessness like sky
reflecting movement like sunlight
reflecting sheet and lace and shawl of clouds
like earth's show of bunchy blossoms
reflecting sun and star glitter
like an everlasting statement of light.

Sea movements want to wash the shore
or just take over all the land.
Oh you sea, you go on reflecting sky,
taking us from land to land –
what sky-reflector restlessness
          what sky-reflector restlessness!

When I Get to Englan

Mother Country

Surrounded by water here
unda pure cloud and sky
consida how when I get to Englan,
come one night, I will dream.

In my dream I have a request to make
to HRH HIS MAJESTY the King.
I will shake his gloved hand,
saying Sar, the Lord has blessed me.

Blessed your subject to look into your eyes
and, Sar, I feel well honoured.
And HRH HIS MAJESTY, King of Britain and Empire,
I have a request to make to you, Sar.

By your Kingdom of the British, my new Mother Country,
you gave me a new name –
and took away my African name
that I carried for generations.

May I request, Sar, kindly, that
you grant me an honour:
that your first grandchild may share
an African name with my first grandchild.

Let him be Prince Kwame!
That, Sar, will truly make me feel
we have been joined by new kinship
that will honour nature and its grand differences –

and will truly ennoble us both.

Wanting to Hear Big Ben

Another traveller said: Man,
me, miself, I wahn go to Englan
specially – fi stan up unda Big Ben

and hear Big Ben a-strike
and feel it there, how
it did echo roun the Whole Worl

and have me rememba, how
when I was a boy passin a radio
playin in a shop, and a-hear

Big Ben a-strike the time,
gongin and vibratin, like it travel
unda centre of earth

or unda the sea
or fram deep-deep sky
and I did kinda feel strange, that

somehow, this mighty echo come fram
a mystery place call centre of mi worl
which I could not imagine at all.

Now – when I get to Landan
I jus wahn to stan-up
unda that striking Big Ben

an man, jus test out
how that vibration work – inside-a-me.

Sociable and Unsociable Ways of Money

A gesturing man said:
Me only goin Englan fi short time
me well si Yankeee Dolla much like
a swanky spreeboy – with wings.
Him is a gambler who will drop in
on a game and put out a bagful
of dollas on the table, piled up high.

And, whereva him is, the eagle
flutta-flutta around everywhere.
And everybody get some Yankee dolla.

But, the Poun – the Poun – is shy.
Especially shy of a black man.
O the Poun is standoffish, hard to meet,
hard to know – like a Lord – evva
a high-walled-away genkleman,
nevva around, like a friend.

Yet – is the ol L-S-D I know.
So, gimme five year in ol Englan
and is all I ask to see me back
there pon the rock of JA, BWI.

All I want is enough L-S-D to stuff me
up, fi me to go back and buy a piece
of five acre lan, to cultivate
and keep me livestock, like say:
jus six cow them, six goat, six pig.
And clean, clean, I forget ol Englan,
America, Canada, or anywhere else.

I tell you, I wahn be around
the dizzy hummin bird
a-flutta in the red hibiscus.

How the Weak Manufactured Power for the Strong

Days washed my generations
like showers of rain that sunk,
vanished in drought,
and we were like rocks.

Rooted in stones and flaming sunlight
the weak worked, and made power for the strong.

Now I go to live with people I helped –
with users of painful power.

I go to live with the unfeeling eaters
who digested the proceeds of my ancestors.
I go driven to fulfil sharing.

I go with bright smiles and awkward speech,
the tree feller, land digger, planter –
the non-harvester.

Awakener of new knowing in the knower
I go to live with faces of elegance and pride –

I who look as if
rooted in stones in sunlight.

Song of Man and Man

Mek me go man –
Mek me go
Mek me go and get
White man look in mi yeye
To challenge each other's wildniss.

Mek me go man –
Mek me go
To face dread and terror
Like white did go face African
Mek me go face white man every day.

Mek dread go man –
Dread go and meet dread
As it wohn be odderwise
Mek me go man
wid salt water behin mi yeye
To bleed away all sorrow.

Mek me go man –
Mek me go
And meet dread in man and man –
That attraction
That could nevva nevva hide.

Mek we go man –
Mek me go
To white man wild sorrow
And black man sorrow what I bring
That sometime
They just melt away togedda.

Mek me go man –
Mek me go
Tiger dohn meet lion
Like lion dohn meet tiger
But man mus meet man
So mek me go man
Mek me go!

Whitehall Goin Turn We Back

      Man oh man
Whitehall order we turn back!
Englan send out warship-them,
warship-them on the way –
warship now face we track,
oh, to drive we back to The Rock.

Who did think we goin go free?
Who did think we have the facility?

Terror races round all decks:
Mother-country goin turn we ship back to sea,
all a-we passenger goin get lock up.
God help we to come close to thee!

Suddenly – a panic of voices:
'British warship a-shadow we!
Oh God, warship a-shadow we.
Them goin bomb we out of the water,
them goin bomb we out of the sea!'

Who did think we goin get there?
Who did believe them goin let we share?

      Man oh man
White people dohn wan black people in Englan.
Now, them goin sink we dead.
White people dohn want we
to mix with the world –
now, them goin sink we dead.

Oh, see – big man-them washed with tears:
Jesas Christ have mercy!
Englan-power goin sink we dead
     to the bottom of the sea
         to the bottom of the sea.

Eatin for Two Man

Man, I eatin fo two man –
everytime, on this ship!
I not landin in Englan
lookin like skeletan.

Man, I eatin fo two man –
everytime, on this ship!
The food is food I nevva eat
so, natural, I a hungry eater.

Man, I eatin fo two man –
everytime, on this ship!
I nyam up steak-and-kidney pie,
tomato soup, beef-stew dinners.

Man, I eatin fo two man –
everytime, on this ship!
Nobody in Englan goin see
I come from hungry-belly history.

Englan Voice

I prepare – an prepare well – fe Englan.
Me decide, and done leave behine
all the voice of ol slave-estate bushman.

None of that distric bad-talk in Englan,
that bush talk of ol slave-estate man.

Hear me speak in Englan, an see
you dohn think I a Englan native.

Me nah go say
'Bwoy, how you du?'
me a-go say 'How are you old man?'

Me nah go say
'Wha yu nyam las night?'
me a-go say 'What did you have for supper?'

Patois talk is bushman talk –
people who talk patois them dam lazy.

Because mi bush voice so settle in me
an might let me down in-a Englan
me a-practise.

Me a-practise talk like teacher
till mi Englan voice come out-a me
like water from hillside rock.

Even if you fellows here
dohn hear mi Englan voice
I have it – an hear it in mi head!

White Suit and White Shoes

1

I movin man, I changin me.
Man – look at me now.
If you have good eyes,
you see notn black.

This White suit me showin off
tonite, is firs whole suit
on mi back. The shoes me wear
is mi firs shoes, mi firs-them, beside
only motor-tyre sandals.

Me goin lan in White Henglan in this
White suit. Notn else will do.
People might know I a show-off
but, nobody will tell me so.

White suit me showin off in
tonite, will introduce Henglan to me
an I think it will introduce me
well – cos it White, and not black.

2

Notice, I dress right fa Henglan.
I must wear notn but White.
A man must not live not-wanted –
must not ignore the taste of his hosts.

I mus keep my teeth clean.
My White teeth must be my focus of attraction.
I will show my teeth White always –
make reassuring grin my full face mask.
Eyes are always on my teeth!

Yes, the White of my eyes and the White of my teeth!
And skin – the dark betrayer – must go in hidin.
The sunny sky that made me black must take it back.
My black face – I left that there in Jamaica.
Let me give it back to Africa!

3

Man – you see me land in White suit –
White suit, White shirt, White shoes.
Even though the shoes is canvas, it White.

Wearing my White shirt, shoes and suit
I will smile smile smile, all the time.

I mus get blue eyes of Henglan
all smilin to see a sunny man
who arrive to get some money
and start to pay the debt
that dress me up White – fa Henglan!

A Greater Oneness

Man, I goin Englan to speed up
what Empire start – that scorn, self-love and pride, I will
put together with humility.

I believe daylight and night-time are partners.
Night covers the day with arms like wings
to leave earth to gestate.

Man, I believe daylight and night-time married
and do proliferate Nature's children –

Man, I see it that all faces of difference
will come together with one face –

walking with multifarious faces,
with love, with peace, with essential growing.

Man, from where this world has come
we cannot be chance-experiment.
We are willing learners and givers
from provisions given.

Man, cruelty is our early wildness
to be more and more tamed
into the untarnished glow of lovingness.

Man – I goin to Englan
to help speed up Englan
into a greater oneness
with an ever growing humanity.

Sea-Song Five

The sea a hot mirror
dances to haze of sky

ships from all the world's corners
criss-cross its face

depths unknown to our seeing
compel our contemplation

those unmeasurable depths
hold fish we can never catch
shells we can never see

the sea is companion to sky
in its sprawling space
and its everchanging light

it gives us moonlight shivering on waves
it gives us darkness, going down, down, down

it has remote distances
that we are pulled to explore

we embrace the sea like mystery –
like depths of our own unknown minds.

PART 3

NEW DAYS ARRIVING

New Space

I lived where the day's light was
a clean and open transparency
so clear I should see into level distances
and, from hilltops,
know every fluttering wing,
every leaf down to the sprawling sea.

I should know every sky glow
and be dreaming in
the white sheeting of moonlight –
moonlight's wide sheeting.

I should be well washed
by clean green spaces and the gargle
of clear and stony streams, invisible
on sheer bird-throated land.

I should sway and echo with
the ancient sea's voice
and its depths, pregnant with life
more varied than the air holds –

longing to stand on the feet of a passing day
        and be carried
                where all new time is stored.

In the Land and Sea Culture-crossed

In the land and sea culture-crossed
we call to the hearts of difference.
Restless, we widen our boundaries.
Expansion may be for self-loving, yet
our world is smaller and closer
and, in gesturing, we touch different other.

A voice in me says:
Completeness comes from
a balance of allness.
All faces and conditions you not
only inherit but with them must find
agreement and oneness.

A voice in me says: Who is not
a beginner, seeking balance?
Who does not want to be heights and depths of music
harmonious with all difference?

A voice in me says:
We will change wildness to love,
into rejuvenation.
There is madness in self-love
we will change it to sanity.
We will release change in each other.

As the ground catches the rotten fruit
for its centre to grow again, and
as only our *negative* selves are hurt by cleansing
for the expansion of self essence,
oh, let us more and more know.

Let us strive for
a coming together of allness in the self,
as, at peace with our centre
inhabiting all faces
inhabiting the core of all centres
being at home with allness
we strive to become habitation of allness.

Beginning in a City, 1948

Stirred by restlessness, pushed by history,
I found myself in the centre of Empire.
Those first few hours, with those packed impressions
I never looked at in all these years.

I knew no room. I knew no Londoner.
I searched without knowing.
I dropped off my grip at the 'left luggage'.
A smart policeman told me a house to try.

In dim-lit streets, war-tired people moved slowly
like dark-coated bears in a snowy region.
I in my Caribbean gear
was a half-finished shack in the cold winds.
In November, the town was a frosty field.
I walked fantastic stone streets in a dream.

A man on duty took my ten-shilling note
for a bed for four nights.
Inflated with happiness I followed him.
I was left in a close-walled room,
left with a dying shadeless bulb,
a pillowless bed and a smelly army blanket –
all the comfort I had paid for.

Curtainless in morning light, I crawled out of bed
onto wooden legs and stiff-armed body,
with a frosty-board face that I patted
with icy water at the lavatory tap.

Then I came to fellow-inmates in a crowded room.
A rage of combined smells attacked me,
clogging my nostrils –
and new charges of other smells merely
increased the stench. I was alone.
I alone was nauseated and choked in deadly air.

One-legged people stood around a wall of hot plates
prodding sizzled bacon and kippers.
Sore-legged and bandaged people poured tea.
Weather-cracked faces, hairy and hairless, were chewing.
No woman smiled. No man chuckled.
Words pressed through gums and gaps of rusty teeth.

Grimy bundles and bags were pets
beside grimy bulges of people, bowed, and in little clusters.
Though ever so gullible I knew – this was a dosshouse.
I collected back seven shillings and sixpence.
I left the place and its smells, their taste still with me
and again instinct directed me.

I walked without map, without knowledge
from Victoria to Brixton. On Coldharbour Lane
I saw a queue of men – some black –
and stopped. I stood by one man in the queue.
'Wha happenin brodda? Wha happenin here?"

Looking at me he said 'You mus be a jus-come?
You did hear about Labour Exchange?' 'Yes – I hear.'
'Well, you at it! But, you need a place whey you live.'
He pointed. 'Go over deie and get a room.'
So, I had begun – begun in London.

Hymn to New Day Arriving

Now – watch this new day arriving,
this glorious world ship coming silently
on the old, old waterway,
bringing the opening of light to seemingly settle.

Oh watch the ancient eye widening
to stir echoes, movements, voices,
to wake up all dormant life,
to tell flowers and faces to open.

Know this day will arouse some peace,
will express vigour to grow,
but, oh, will unleash merciless debt callers,
will corrode the energy of love.

Oh think of sweet first loves that will rot
and those that will flame like bright leaves.
Think of the finished work, standing like a building,
and the empty work that drains out hope.

New day is a turned-over book page,
new day renews spirit of energy.
Just like a little fresh cool breeze
new day invigorates with new life.

Then remember this
is only another day arriving,
coming with its new arousals
and despatching lives of completed time.

Oh how everything has its movement, its voice, its ending –
it is overwhelming.

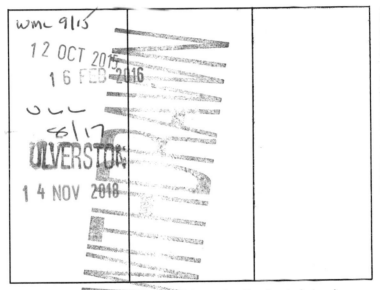
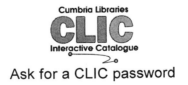

WRITING
BUSINESS AND PERSONAL
LETTERS

Robert Fry

www.straightforwardco.co.uk

Straightforward Guides

© Straightforward Publishing 2015

British cataloguing in publication data. A catalogue record of this book is available from the British Library.

ISBN: 9781847165466

Printed and bound by 4edge Ltd www.4edge.co.uk

Cover Design by Bookworks Islington.

CONTENTS

Introduction

PART 1 – THE IMPORTANCE OF LANGUAGE.

Introduction

This book is a brief introduction to the art of letter writing. After long deliberation, I decided not to produce a book full of standard letters for the reader to copy rote fashion. Although many books of this nature do exist, there seems no point in merely allowing the reader to copy someone else's work.

The main point when producing letters is that the writer must understand the very essence of the language in which he or she is writing. This involves understanding grammar and punctuation – in short understanding the basis of the language, in this case the English language.

Mastery of language and the ability to express oneself, in the business or personal domains, is a wonderful achievement. Mastery and effective use of language is akin to painting a beautiful picture.

This book dwells at the outset on grammar and punctuation and other finer points of the language. It shows the writer of the business or personal letter how to express what it is they are trying to say, how to lay it out and how to take care that the letter achieves its aim.

This little book is rigorous but rewarding. It does not seek to layout 50 different types of letter but to show the reader how to understand the complexities of the language and to coach the reader into a position where he or she will begin to enjoy the language more and to produce an effective letter, whether of a personal or business nature.

****

PART 1.

THE IMPORTANCE OF LANGUAGE

Ch. 1

The Importance of Punctuation

There are a number of essential elements key to effective letter writing, whether business or personal letters. Basic punctuation is extremely important.

Consider how you speak to someone. Generally, what you say is not one long breathless statement. It is punctuated by full stops. When writing, think about how you would verbalise the same statement and insert full stops as appropriate. For example:

We went walking today and we stopped at a shop and bought something to eat and sat down and ate the food and then decided to move on we walked as far as we could before deciding to sit down and take a rest after half an hour we then decided to turn back-------

Immediately, it is obvious that this statement is one long sentence which would leave the listener, or in turn the reader, confused. The correct version might be:

We went walking today, and we stopped at a shop and bought something to eat. We sat down and ate the food and then decided to walk on. We walked as far as we could before deciding to sit down and take a rest. After half an hour we decide to turn back-

The main point is that by inserting full stops we add structure to a sentence.

The use of commas

Whilst full stops are very important in order to add structure and also to separate out one sentence from the next, sometimes there can be a tendency to use commas instead of full stops. Commas have a particular role but can never take the place of full stops.

Commas are used to add a pause to a statement before concluding with a full stop. They are also used to separate items in a list. When using commas to separate items in a list the last one must be preceded by 'and'.

For example:
Dave liked swimming, football, ice hockey, mountain climbing, fell walking *and* judo.

Another example:
Peter was preparing his homework for the next day, his mother was cooking, his father was reading the paper *and* his sister was listening to music.

Beginning a sentence with a conjunction (joining word)

If you begin a sentence with a conjunction (joining word,) put a comma to separate the first part of the sentence from the rest of it. In this sentence, 'if' is a joining word and there is a comma after 'word'.

Here are two more examples with the conjunction underlined. Notice where the comma is placed:

Because it was snowing, we decided to stay inside.
As the sun set, the sky glowed.

Commas are used to separate groups of words within a sentence, in order to give statements within sentences more emphasis. Commas are used in many other areas too, such as before a question (I am not sure about that, are you?) or before a name (do be silent, Jack).

The most important element here, as with full stops, is that when you are composing a letter, think about what you are saying, to whom you are addressing it, and take time to punctuate the statement. This means that the person reading the letter can immediately relate to the contents and can interpret the message.

Making use of semi-colons, colons and the dash

The semi-colon is a very useful punctuation mark. It can be used when you feel that you do not need a full stop; usually the

17

second statement follows closely to the first one. A capital letter is not used after a semi-colon. For example:

The road was getting busier; it was obvious that the traffic was starting to build up.

The idea of traffic building up follows on naturally from the road getting busier. In this case, it might be tempting to use a comma. However, as both statements follow on so closely a semi-colon is more appropriate.

The colon

A colon can be used for two purposes. It can introduce a list of statements, as in the following example:

There are two reasons why you failed: you lost your way, it was dark and you did not follow my orders.

Like the semi-colon you need no capital letter after the colon. The colon can also be used to show two statements reinforcing each other:
Your general punctuation is weak: you must learn to use the full stop and comma more effectively.

Using the dash

A dash is used for emphasis. What is said between dashes – or after the dash if there is only one – is more emphatic than if there were no dash. If you break your sentence in the middle to make an added point, use a dash before and after it:

Peter, Dave, Fred Grace – in fact everyone – had decided to go.

Use of the question mark

We have considered full stops, commas, semi-colons, colons and the use of the dash. We now need to consider the question mark.

The question mark is obviously placed at the end of the question. You should always remember to include the question mark as, if it is missed, the reader of a letter might not take your question to be a question, but a statement.

Example

Is it raining outside?

You are not intending to go out in this weather, are you?

The second question is clearly a mixture of statement and question. To be understood as a question it is important to insert a question mark at the end. If you are using direct speech, the question mark takes the place of the comma and is always placed inside the inverted commas (speech marks):

'When are you going?' asked Susan.

Use of exclamation marks

The exclamation mark should be used rarely otherwise it loses its impact. It should not be used for emphasis; your choice of words should be sufficient to provide the necessary emphasis. It is used in direct speech, again in place of a comma. There should always be an exclamation mark if the word 'exclaimed' is used: 'I cannot believe you said that! She exclaimed.

Putting punctuation into practice.

Having discussed very basic punctuation, the main elements of which you will always use in letters, it is time to do a basic exercise.

Punctuate the following:

1. Dave was very angry with the garage he had bought the car from them and they had stated that the car was in perfect condition at least they had said that he would have no problem with it the car had been nothing but a problem and now he had lost his rag and decided to confront the owner and try to get his money or some of it back.
2. I don't think that is true she exclaimed
What don't you think is true he said?
It cannot be true that every time I go out I see the same person following me he seems to know my exact movements and I am very worried now.
   3. I feel that I am knocking my head against a brick wall I have asked my mother father brother and sister what they think of my

painting I felt that I had to ask them all by the way and all of them ignored me its as if I have offended them or something or they are to embarrassed to comment.

Now read the key points from Chapter 1.

****

Key points from Chapter 1

- Basic punctuation is one of the most important elements of effective letter writing.

- By inserting elements of punctuation we add structure to our letter.

- Whilst full stops are used to add structure, commas are used to add a pause and emphasis to a statement.

- Make effective use of colons, semi-colons and dashes.

- Question marks and exclamation marks must only be used when asking a question or adding emphasis.

Ch. 2

The Importance of Grammar

Making use of your sentence

Using nouns correctly

Nouns are a list of 'things'. The following are typical nouns: car, clock, computer, mechanic, spanners, and so on.

Each of the above words can be the subject of a sentence if it is linked to a verb:

The garage *was* closed

The mechanic *arrived* late

The clock *fell* off the wall

The noun is the subject of the sentence and the verb, which is italicised in the above brief statements, is the doing word. A noun must be linked to a verb if it is to make sense.

Using verbs correctly

A verb is a 'doing' or 'being' word. There must be at least one verb in a sentence otherwise it is not a sentence.

Understanding verbs

Verbs can be either finite or non-finite.

Finite verbs

Finite verbs must show tense. They can be past, present or future and are always connected to a noun or pronoun. (more about pronouns later.)

Consider the verbs and tenses in the following statements:

Tomorrow I will travel to Bristol

Yesterday she was unhappy

He plays the guitar extremely well

'will travel' is the future tense.

'was' is the past tense.
'plays' is the present tense.

Non-finite verbs
The non-finite verbs are the infinitive form of the verb and the present and past participles.

The infinitive
The infinitive is the form of verb that has 'to' before it:

To run, to sing, to eat, to walk.

Many people consider it incorrect to use a 'split infinitive'. This is when a word is placed between the 'to' and the verb:

It is difficult *to* accurately *assess* the data
The following example is better. The infinitive 'to assess' has not been 'split' by the adverb 'accurately'

It is difficult accurately *to assess* the data.

Past participles

The past participle is used with the verb 'to have'; it then forms a finite verb. Either the present or the past tense of the verb 'to have' can be used. It will depend on the context. Look at the following examples. The past participles are italicised:
She had *scratched* her leg.

He has *passed* his driving test.

David has *prepared* supper.

Peter had *written* a letter to his father.
The first three participles in the examples above are the same as the ordinary past tense but 'has' or 'had' have been added. In the last example the past participle 'written' is different and can only be used with the verb 'to have'.

Present participle
The present participle always ends in '-ing' and is introduced by the verb 'to be'. The past or present tense of the verb 'to be' can be used:

David is *helping* his mother.

Susan was *washing* the car.

Using the gerund
The present principle can also be used as a noun. In this case it is called a gerund:

Shopping is fun.
The *wailing* was continuous.

Using the present participle as an adjective
Certain present participles can also be used as adjectives:

The *crying* child ran to its mother.

The *howling* dog kept the family awake.

Now look at the following examples:

Rushed across the road.
Came into the shop.

Are these sentences? Of course they are not. Although they each have a verb, they have no subject linked to them. We don't know who rushed across the road or came into the shop. Add a noun and it makes sense:

The dog rushed across the road

The woman came into the shop.

In each sentence there must be a noun which is linked to a verb.

The above represents basic grammar, which, if linked with correct punctuation, helps you to structure a coherent and understandable letter that will be readily understood and will also instil a certain respect in the reader. If you require a more intense introduction to grammar there are a number of useful books on the market. Many colleges also run courses.

Paragraphing letters

Look at the following example:

John was very used to intimidating others. Every Saturday he would go into the local pub, sit there patiently until his friends started to drift in, and then begin hectoring them and generally 'winding them up'. Johns friends were very used to this and they put up with it because they knew him of old and, in many cases, gave as good as they got. One day, however, John sat as usual in the pub and he noticed that none of his friends had appeared, as was the norm. Another hour passed and still they had not showed up. John phoned Dave on his mobile. Dave answered and he stated that he was fed up with Johns hectoring, as were his friends. John wondered what to do in the face of the rejection of his friends. He was worried and it caused him to reflect on his behaviour. He came to the conclusion that he should visit them and discuss the problem.

The above is one long sentence, which should be broken into paragraphs. Paragraphs can vary into length but each paragraph deals with one topic. The positioning of the topic sentence can vary. The following example shows the above in paragraph form:

John was very used to intimidating others. Every Saturday he would go into the local pub, sit there patiently until his friends started to drift in, and then begin hectoring them and generally 'winding them up'. Johns friends were very used to this and they put up with it because they knew him of old and, in many cases, gave as good as they got.

One day, however, John sat as usual in the pub and he noticed that none of his friends had appeared, as was the norm. Another hour passed and still they had not showed up. John phoned Dave on his mobile. Dave answered and he stated that he was fed up with Johns hectoring, as were his friends. John wondered what to do in the face of the rejection of his friends. He was worried and it caused him to reflect on his behaviour. He came to the conclusion that he should visit them and discuss the problem.

Using quotation marks

Inverted commas are also used to enclose quotations and titles: She went to the cinema to see the film 'Star wars'.

'A stitch in time saves nine' is a famous proverb.

The expression 'of the minds eye' comes from Shakespeare's play 'Hamlet'.

Notice that the full stop has been placed outside the inverted commas when the quotation or title is at the end of the sentence.

Now read the key points from Chapter 2, Grammar.

****

Key points from Chapter 2

- Nouns are a list of things, a verb is a doing word.

- There must be at least one verb in a sentence otherwise it is not a sentence.

- Verbs can be either finite or non-finite.

- The past participle is used with the verb 'to have'.

- The present participle always ends in '-ing' and is introduced by the verb 'to be'.

- By paragraphing letters you break down the flow of writing and introduce structure.

Ch. 3

Spelling

English spelling is not easy to learn. There are, of course, some rules. However, there are exceptions to these rules. Some spelling and pronunciation appear to be illogical. It is therefore very important that certain spellings are learnt.

There are 26 letters in the English alphabet. Five are vowels and the rest are consonants.

Forming words

The vowels are A,E,I,O,U. All words have to contain at least one vowel ('Y' is considered to be a vowel in words like 'rhythm' and 'psychology') Consonants are all the other letters that are not vowels. So that a word can be pronounced easily, vowels are placed between them. No more than three consonants can be placed together. Below are two lists. The first contains some words with three consecutive consonants and the second are words with two consecutive consonants:

(a) school, scream, chronic, Christian, through, splash.
(b) Flap, grab, occasion, commander, baggage, added.

All the words in the examples have the consonants separated by vowels.

Forming plurals

To form a plural word an 's' is usually added to a noun. There are some exceptions. If a noun ends in 'y' and there is a consonant before it, a plural is formed by changing the 'y' into an 'i' and adding '-ies':

Lady = ladies
nappy = nappies
company = companies
berry = berries

If the 'y' is preceded by another vowel, an 's' only is added:

monkey = monkeys
donkey = donkeys
covey = coveys

If a noun ends in 'o' and a consonant precedes the 'o', '-es' is added to form a plural:

potato = potatoes
tomato = tomatoes
hero = heroes

If there is a vowel before the 'o' an 's' only is added:

studio = studios
zoo = zoos
patio = patios

Changing the form of a verb

When a verb ends in 'y' and it is necessary to change the tense by adding other letters, the 'y' is changed into an 'i' and 'es' or 'ed' is added:

He will *marry* her tomorrow

He was *married* yesterday

A dog likes to *bury* his bone

A dog always *buries* his bone

Using long vowels and short vowels

There is often a silent 'e' at the end of the word if the vowel is 'long':
Date, bite, hope, late, dupe.

Each of these words consists of one syllable (one unit of sound) if another is added, the 'e' is removed:
Date = dating
Bite = biting
And so on.

Adding '-ly' to adjectives
When forming an adverb from an adjective 'ly' (not ley) is added. If there is a 'y' at the end of the adjective, it must be changed to an 'i':

Adjective	*Adverb*
Happy	Happily
Beautiful	Beautifully
Quick	Quickly
Slow	Slowly

'I' before 'e' except after 'c'.

This rule seems to have been made to be broken. Some words keep to it but some break it. Here are some that follow the rule. All of them are pronounced 'ee' – as in 'seed':

No 'c' in front	*After 'c'*
niece	ceiling
piece	receive
grief	deceive

Exceptions to this rule are:

Neighbours, vein, either, neither, seize, weird.

Using a dictionary
Checking your spelling
Use a dictionary frequently to check your spelling. Don't guess the spelling of a word. Look it up. It is helpful to keep a list of words that you have misspelled so that you can learn them.

Looking at words

A dictionary not only tells you how to spell a word. It also tells you what part of speech the word is. Sometimes the word appears more than once as it has different meanings and can be used as a different part of speech. Look at the following examples:

Land (noun)   (a)   The solid part of the earth
               (b)   A country

Land (verb)

(c) To go ashore or bring a plane down to the ground

The dictionary will also often give the derivation of a word. English is a rich language that owes much to other languages. If you have time, browse through a dictionary looking at the derivation of some of the words. It can be a fascinating experience.

Making use of the thesaurus

A thesaurus can be very useful. It will help you to find an alternative word (synonym) for a word that you have used too much. Words are shown alphabetically and beside each will be a list of words that could replace the word that you want to lose. Not all synonyms will be suitable. It depends on the context of the word.

Now read the key points from Chapter 3, spelling, overleaf.

Key points from Chapter 3

- There are 26 letters in the English alphabet, 5 are vowels and the rest consonants.

- Every word has a vowel

- No more than three consonants can be placed together.

- Use a dictionary frequently to check your spelling.

- A thesaurus will provide many alternatives to a word.

Ch. 4

Apostrophes and Abbreviations

Using apostrophes to show possession

Apostrophes are put at the end of nouns when the nouns have something belonging to them.

Making a singular noun possessive

If a noun is singular and it has something belonging to it, add an apostrophe and an 's'. For singular words that show possession the apostrophe is always placed before the 's':

Karen's handbag was stolen.
Her neighbour's fence was blown down.
The child's ball bounced over the wall.

If the singular noun already ends in an 's' another 's' should still be added:

The princess's bridal gown was made by a well-known couturier.
The thief stole the Duchess's jewels.

However, in some cases, the extra 's' can be omitted as in the following cases:

James' book was missing
He damaged his Achilles' tendon.

Making a plural noun possessive

Most nouns add an 's' to make a plural. In this case the apostrophe goes after the noun if it is possessive:

The thundering of the horses' hoofs broke the silence.
The ladies' gowns were beautiful.

Some nouns do not add an 's' to become a plural. In this case, if they are possessive, they are treated like singular nouns. The apostrophe is added before the extra 's'. Some of these words are: children, men, women, mice, sheep, geese:

The children's playground was vandalised.

Kate watched the mice's tails disappearing round the corner.

Using possessive pronouns correctly

When using the possessive form of a pronoun, apostrophes are not used. The possessive pronouns are: mine, her, his, its, ours, yours and theirs.

The blame is mine (no apostrophe)
These books are hers (no apostrophe)
The first prize was his (no apostrophe)

Abbreviating words

When writing formally, it is better not to abbreviate. Write the words out in full. However, it is, of course, acceptable to abbreviate when writing dialogue.

Using apostrophes to abbreviate words

An abbreviation is when letters are missed out. Sometimes two words are combined into one. An apostrophe is placed where the letter or letters have been omitted:

'Do not' = don't
'Can not' = can't
'Would not' = wouldn't

Note especially that 'Could have' becomes 'could've' not 'could of'. Because of the way the abbreviation in the above example sounds, a common mistake is to use the word 'of' instead of the abbreviation 've'.

Abbreviating words without using apostrophes
When words are shortened, it is usual to put a full stop at the end:
information   info.
document   doc.
etcetera   etc.

The names of counties are shortened in the same way and all have full stops after them:

39

Berkshire Berks.
Nottinghamshire Notts.

Other words that are often abbreviated are titles but some of these should only be abbreviated if the title is followed by the person's full name. A full stop should be put after the abbreviation if it is used:

Capt. Edward Symes
not
Capt. Symes

Handling contractions

Some words are abbreviated by using the first and last letters only. These are contractions of the original word and do not usually need a full stop at the end:

Mister   Mr
Mistress Mrs
Doctor   Dr
No full stop is needed after a contraction.

Using acronyms

It is becoming increasingly common to describe companies or organisations only by the initial letters of the names of the group. This is called an acronym. This is now so prevalent that we often forget what the original letters stood for. It is no longer considered necessary to put a full stop after each capital letter. Here are some reminders of frequently used acronyms:

RADA   Royal Academy of Dramatic Arts
NATO   North Atlantic Treaty Organisation
ASH   Action on Smoking and Health
UNICEF United Nations Children's Fund
RAF   Royal Air Force
And many more!

Now read the key points from Chapter 4, apostrophes and abbreviations.

****

Key points from Chapter 4

- Apostrophes are put at the end of nouns when the nouns have something belonging to them.

- If a noun is singular and it has something belonging to it, add an apostrophe and an 's'. For singular words that show possession the apostrophe is always placed before the 's.

- Most nouns add an 's' to make a plural. In this case the apostrophe goes after the 's' if it is possessive.

- When writing formally, it is better not to abbreviate.

- It is becoming more popular to use acronyms to abbreviate companies or organisations.

Ch. 5

Using the Correct English

Recognising common mistakes

Remember that punctuation is essential if your work is to make sense.

- Do not use commas instead of full stops. If in doubt, put a full stop.
- Remember to put a question mark at the end of a question.

Revising sentence construction

Remember that sentences must make sense. Each sentence must contain at least one subject (noun) and one verb. If there is more than one verb, there are two clauses and these should either be separated by a full stop or a semi-colon or linked by a conjunction.

Revising the correct use of verbs

Always make sure that the nouns and verbs 'agree'. If the noun is singular, the verb should always be singular. Remember that collective nouns are singular and are followed by the singular form of the verb.

The politician is hoping to win tonight.

not

The politician *are* hoping to win tonight.

Avoiding the misuse of pronouns

There is often confusion in the words 'I' and 'me', 'she' and 'her', 'he' and 'him', 'we' and 'us', 'they' and 'them'.

'I', 'she', 'he', 'we', and 'they', are personal pronouns and are usually the subject of the sentence. This means they are the instigators of the action in the sentence:

I like travelling
*Sh*e went on holiday
He went home
We have no bread
They are going today

'Me, 'her', 'him', 'us', and 'them', are usually the objects of the sentence. This means that something is done to them:

The stone hit *me*
The prize was given to *her*
The wall collapsed on *him*
The dog bit *us*
The mother scolded *them*

Revising spelling

- Learn the most commonly misspelled words; for example:

Surprise, disappear, disappoint, independent

- Learn the correct spelling of words that sound the same but are spelt differently; for example:

hear - here
their - there
sea - see
too - two - to

The words 'practice' and 'practise' are often confused and so are 'advice' and 'advise'. 'Practise' and 'advise' are the verbs and 'practice' and 'advice' are the nouns:

You must practise the guitar if you are to improve.
There is a cricket practice at the net today.
I advise you not to do that
Please take my advice.

Other words that are often confused are 'council' and 'counsel', 'compliment' and 'compliment', 'principle' and 'principal' and 'stationery' and 'stationary'.

Avoiding common mistakes

A mistake that is often heard is the following:

He is very different *to* his brother.

This is not correct and should read:

He is very different *from* his brother.

If you **differ,** you move away from. If you are **similar** you are similar to.

Avoiding mistakes when using apostrophes and abbreviations

- Do not put an apostrophe every time there is a plural word ending in 's'.
- The abbreviation of 'could have' is 'could've' not 'could of'.
- Do not put a full stop after a contraction:

Doctor - Dr
Mister - Mr

Avoiding unnecessary repetition

- Remember that nouns do not usually need to be repeated within the same sentence.
- Replace them with pronouns

He tried on his new boots. The boots were too tight.

This should be:
He tried on his new boots. *They* were too tight.

46

Avoiding tautologies

A tautology is where the same thing is said twice over in different ways, for example:

The last chapter will be at the end of the book.
The people applauded by clapping their hands.

These two sentences are repetitious. The meaning is at the beginning of the sentence and has been repeated again at the end. Avoid tautologies.

Varying the sentence

If sentences frequently begin with the same word, the word becomes monotonous. Avoid the temptation to start consecutive sentences in the same way.

She went to the car. She opened the trunk. She closed the trunk. She was upset.

These sentences all start with she so the passage does not flow. It is easy to say the same thing in another way so that it does flow:

Susan went to the car and opened the trunk. Closing the trunk, she was clearly upset.

Making comparisons
When using adjectives to compare two things or people '-er' is usually added to the base word:

47

big   bigger
tall   taller
slow   slower
happy   happier

When more than two people are involved, '-est' is added to the adjective:

Big   bigger   biggest
Tall   taller   tallest
Slow slower   slowest

Some words are so constructed that to add the suffix '-er' or '-est' would produce clumsy words. In this case 'more' and 'most' are put before the adjective instead:

beautiful   more beautiful   most beautiful

intelligent more intelligent   most intelligent

Eliminating jargon

The word 'jargon' derives from a Middle English word meaning 'meaningless chatter'. The derivation suggests a very good reason why jargon should be avoided. Anyone who is a member of a group uses jargon that is intelligible only to other members of the same group.

Lawyers have their own jargon and so do politicians, schoolteachers and nurses.

You should use words and expressions that can be easily understood by all and not forms of language that have grown up around professions, for example, as these can often serve to confuse unless you are part of that group.

An example of such words can be words that end in 'ise'. Privatise, normalise, prioritise and so on. Make sure that you use language which is not restricted and is in common use.

Avoiding clichés

Clichés are phrases that are heard over and over again. We all use them and they are often very apt.

Creating similes

'White as a sheet' and 'ran like the wind' are similes. These are comparisons between two things using the words 'like' or 'as'. Many clichés are similes and they are often very vivid. However, they are not original and you should avoid them.

Using metaphors

Metaphors are also comparisons but they are 'implied' and do not use 'like' or 'as'. We use metaphorical language a great deal in everyday speech. It is language that is not literally true but cannot be classified as a lie as everyone knows what is meant.

Look at the following examples:
I'm starving.

He says he's freezing
She's dying of thirst.

All are clichés and all are metaphors. The language is metaphorical – not literally true. If it were true, all three characters would be dead and we know that is not what is meant.

Improving your style
Economising on words

Good writing is simple and easy to understand. Unnecessary words should be eliminated. If one word can replace four then use it.

Using the active voice

The active voice is more positive than the passive voice. In the active voice a subject does something. In the passive voice something is done to him.

Active voice

The father struck his son
The teacher gave his class a detention

Passive voice

The son was struck by his father
The class was given a detention by the teacher

Avoiding negatives

Using positive statements instead of negative ones also economises on words. For example:
He did not remember his wife's birthday.
Clare was not present in the afternoon.

Would be better as the following:

He forgot his wife's birthday
Clare was absent in the afternoon.

Avoid double negatives which make a positive:

There isn't no one there
I haven't got no lunch

The word 'not' and 'no' cancel each other out and therefore the first example means that there is someone there and the second means that I have got lunch.

There is a choice of two correct versions. Only one negative should be used if the sense is to be kept:

There isn't anyone there.
Or

There is no one there.
I haven't got any lunch.
or
I have no lunch.

Developing your own style

By now you should have a good grasp of the basics of English and you should aim to develop your own style of writing. Avoid repetition and vary your sentences. Look at a cross section of other people's styles and begin to develop a style of your own. The art of writing is a very satisfying art, particularly when done with care and attention.

Now read the key points from Chapter 5 overleaf.

****

Key points from Chapter 5.

- Do not use commas instead of full stops. If in doubt put a full stop.

- Each sentence must contain at least one noun and one verb.

- Avoid the misuse of pronouns.

- Learn the most commonly misspelled words.

- Avoid common mistakes.

- Avoid unnecessary repetition.

- Avoid tautologies.

- Try to vary sentences.

- Eliminate jargon and avoid clichés.

- Economise on words.

- Develop your own style.

PART 2
WRITING LETTERS

Ch. 6

Writing Business Letters

Having studied the basics of English grammar, it is now time to construct an effective letter.

Aiming your letter

Letters project images of you and your organisation to the broad outside world. Clients and general customers of your business will build up a picture of you and your organisation from the style of letter that you write.

When you write a letter you should consider to whom you are addressing it. What is the aim of your letter? A clear aim will tell the reader what he or she wishes to know, but also helps you as a writer by telling you what you do not need to write.

A letter provides a permanent record of transactions between organisations. That record will guide future actions and may also appear as evidence in cases where contractual problems are arising and court action is necessary. Your record must be clear and correct.

Ask why you are writing and then you can focus on what your letter is aiming to achieve:
- payment of an overdue account

- sales of a new product
- technical information
- confirmation of a meeting

Who is your reader?

You should give thought to the person who will read your letter. For incoming letters seek guidance from:

- the name of the job or department title at the end
- the content of the letter

If you are initiating correspondence, make sure that you have targeted your reader accurately. It might be worth making a telephone call to ask who deals with a certain area. Once you have done this you can direct your request to the most appropriate person. Buyer and salesman have a different outlook on a similar product. In making a technical enquiry to the buyer you will expect a competent reply: the salesman's competence may direct you to the benefit of buying the product.

One very important point is that the level of your writing must be your natural way of expressing your meaning. If you try to adopt any other style than the one that is natural to you, you will emerge as strained and unnatural.

What does your reader need?

When you respond to a letter, take a close look at what it requires:

- Is it looking for information?
- Does it need action?
- What action does it require and by when?

Consider how to approach the task

Writing acts as a window through which the reader may see the personality that lies behind the words. In certain cases, this can be a disadvantage, for example if you have an indifferent attitude or if other factors have influenced your mood. This will be reflected in the letter. You have to remember that when people read letters they will pick up varied messages, depending on their own personality and your mood and style when writing the letter.

There are advantages. Once that you are aware that your attitude shows in your writing then you can use this to considerable effect. Do not try to hide your personality, let the reader see that you are able to understand the readers problems, that you are willing to help or that you are patient if a mistake has been made or incomplete information has been given.

Your approach will obviously vary considerably depending on who you are writing to. If you are writing to complain about poor service you will expect to be firm in your tone. You are likely to be plain speaking, specifying what is wrong and laying out timescales for action.

If you are writing in reply to a complaint from a customer, a firm approach will be inappropriate. You will need to adopt a different, more conciliatory approach.

In professional firms, letters rarely go beyond the conventional picture of three short paragraphs. These letters may be:

- offering advice of some sort, such as financial advice
- specifying an architects detailed requirements for progress on a job

In handling more extended material you will need a more complete and visible classification of the content. This will show in headings, and perhaps sub-headings within the narrative, to give the required direction to the reader.

Decide where and when to write
The place and timing of your letter is critical. The reader will not be very happy if your letter arrives on the morning that a crucial decision has to be made, a decision which will be influenced by your letter. Neither will that person be happy if the letter goes to the wrong address. This can easily happen where businesses are organised around different addresses. Your sales letter must arrive at the time that relates to the budget, or the buying decision. At the same time it must be persuasive enough to encourage the reader to put it on record in anticipation of such a time.

Now read the key points from Chapter Six, Writing Business Letters.

Key points from Chapter Six

- Letters project images of you and the organisation to the outside world.

- When you write a letter, you should consider to whom you are addressing it.

- A letter provides a permanent record of transactions between organisations.

- Decide when and where to write a letter.

Ch. 7

Planning and Structuring a Letter

Many people who write letters do so in a hurry and will not give a great amount of time or thought to the contents. In some cases, this may be suitable, especially if you are writing a very short letter of acknowledgement. However, in longer business letters that require more elaboration, then this is not appropriate and a great deal more thought needs to be exercised.

A relatively small amount of time is needed to plan and write letters and, in the long run, will save you time and effort. A well-planned letter will ensure that you communicate the right amount of information and detail to the reader.

Many writers sometimes have problems with the opening sentence of a letter. There is the idea that the opening sentence is of the utmost importance and that the rest will flow easily. This is not always the case. When planning a letter, work from the general to the particular. The detail will then tend to fall naturally into place.

The contents of your letter

When determining the content of your letter, you should ask yourself:
- who is my reader?
- What does that person need to know?

If that person needs to know very little, for example that you intend to be at a meeting, a few words will suffice. However, if the person wishes to know quite a lot then you will need to be very methodical in planning the contents of the letter. When approaching such a task:

- gather relevant information
- allocate the information to main sections
- give each main section a heading

With classification it is tempting to choose general or abstract headings that allow the detail to fit comfortably. You will achieve a better result by choosing more selective, more concrete headings.

Decide the sequence of delivery

It is difficult to think about the content of your letter without giving thought to the sequence in which you will deliver it. A natural order will quite often emerge.

When you are resolving a problem:

- what has gone wrong
- why it went wrong
- what will we do to put it right

When you review activity:
- what we have done in the past
- how we operate currently

- what we plan for the future

A natural order promotes a logical flow of thinking and allows the letter to end at the point you wish to reach:

- looking ahead rather than looking back
- solving a problem rather than raising one

For more complicated letters people tend to group their material functionally but find the sequence more challenging and often repeat material. To plan your sequence:

- spread your headings across the top of a sheet of A4 using the landscape or horizontal plane.
- List the points that relate to each heading in columns
- Consider any changes in the sequence
- Decide whether larger sections should break down into sub-headings or whether additional headings would be better.

An outline classification can show your intended approach to a colleague or other. Changes are easy to make and the outline classification will serve as an excellent prompt for your draft letter.

Forming paragraph structure

We discussed paragraph structures earlier on. There are no rules for paragraphing that require text to be broken after a certain number of words or line. Paragraphs have a lot more to do with consistency of thought than length. However, there are guidelines that help to convert planned content into readable paragraphs:

- change paragraph with each change of subject
- if your subject requires lengthy exploration, break it into further paragraphs that reflect the different aspects.
- Headline your paragraph to give an early indication of your subject.

Many business letters are brief and to the point and can be delivered in a single paragraph. The key is to ensure that the reader can follow your train of thought and that your letter is not one long rambling monologue.

Many single page business letters appear in a three-paragraph format that reflects:

- identification
- explanation
- action

In these cases the opening and closing paragraphs are often short – commonly a single sentence. The middle paragraph expands to the extent that it is necessary to complete.

Paragraph length is also about a particular writing style. A single sentence can make an emphatic paragraph but over-use of single sentence paragraphs will diminish their effect.

Control your sentence length

Writers struggling to construct a sentence are usually concerned with finding the right words to convey their intended meaning to the reader. You should avoid the long lead-in to a sentence. Your lead-in should be snappy and direct as opposed to long winded. If you find it difficult to express your thoughts you should think to yourself, what exactly am I trying to say?

Researchers have measured writing to see what makes it readable. Answers usually include the types of words used and the sentence length. The ideal sentence length is usually about twenty words. After this a sentence can tend to become unwieldy.

Words are not just counted between full stops: the colon and semi-colon also determine the sentence structure for this purpose.

You should remember that you are seeking a readable average sentence length: you are not trying to make every sentence twenty words long. Variety in sentence length will produce a more interesting style. You should adopt a conversational approach in your writing, controlling your sentence length.

Use a range of punctuation

Again, in chapter 2, we looked at punctuation generally. Relating this directly to letter writing, the trend is to use only the punctuation you need to reveal your meaning.

The full stop

A sentence must contain a subject and a finite verb; a finite verb is a verb that has been modified by its subject.

A sentence must express a complete thought but can have a very simple structure:

David writes
It is snowing

Semicolon

The semicolon provides a useful pause, lighter than the full stop but heavier than a comma. You will use it most reliably by ensuring that the elements you have linked could appear as independent sentences.

Colon

Many writers in business use the colon to introduce a list:

During the recent visit to the exhibition, the following items were lost: one briefcase, one wallet, one umbrella and a set of keys.

The colon also allows you to define or illustrate an initial statement:

Following my operation, my personal circumstances changed somewhat: I found myself short of money and unable to work.

Commas

There are many technical reasons for using commas but these are mainly to do with building a pause to indicate your meaning on first reading.

- use a comma when you wish to indicate such a pause
- do not break a sentence, unnecessarily with a comma.
- Do not use a comma if you need a heavier stop, this section applies even if the next point is linked. (a semi-colon should replace the comma here).

Brackets

Brackets enclose an aside or illustration and need no further punctuation.

There are 5280 feet (or 1760 yards) in a mile

It is useful for husband and wife (in certain circumstances) to hold a joint bank account.

Question marks

Use question marks only for direct questions.

Where are you going?
When are you going to send the cheque?

Now read the key points from Chapter Seven overleaf

****

Key points from Chapter Seven

- Business letters cannot, usually, be written in a hurry. This is especially the case if they are longer letters trying to convey complex information.

- When planning a letter, work from the general to the particular.

- When determining the contents of a letter, you should ask who is your reader and what do they need to know.

- Decide the sequence of delivery.

- Structure your letter.

- Control your sentence length.

- Use a range of punctuation.

Ch. 8

Layout of Letters

Letters always have a certain convention that distinguishes them from e-mail and memorandum. Letters always begin 'Dear...........' and end 'Yours sincerely..........'. This is the same whatever the nature and tone of the letter, whether you are writing a strong letter of complaint or a more measured letter.

However, letters have become less formal and word processing now gives many more options for the alignment and appearance of text than a layout that was once dictated by the limitations of a typewriter.

The majority of letters are left aligned only, leaving a ragged right margin that appears less formal and aids reading. Key information such as the reference, date, address, salutation, complimentary close and enclosures is increasingly aligned to the left margin.

Letterheads have changed too. Once all information appeared at the top of the page. Now you may see the company logo prominent at the top but much of the statutory detail at the foot.

Quote references in full
We put a reference on a letter so that when someone replies quoting the reference, we are easily able to find the letter on file. Always quote a reference when replying. Much correspondence

is stored electronically and the quoted reference may be the only manageable way of retrieving a particular letter.

One common layout will begin:

Reference
Date
Address of reader
....
....

An alternative layout will show:

Address of reader   Your ref:
                                           Our ref:
....   Date:
....
....

In the second example, the information will often appear in print on the company letterhead and the position will reflect the letter template on the word processor.

You should look at the address not simply to direct your letter to the receiving organisation but to the individual from whom you seek a response. It is now usual practice to include the name and job title of the recipient as part of the address. As that information appears through the window of the envelope your information can be targeted unopened to the reader.

Choose an appropriate salutation

Try to include the name in the salutation at the start of your letter. This will:

- get commitment from a reader whom you have targeted precisely
- set a personal tone for your writing

Writers sometimes identify themselves with just name and initials at the end of a letter. However, there is a practical problem in that we need to attach a style (Mr Mrs Miss Ms) to the reply.

Very formal style still appears in business letters. You may find a letter that begins:

(See overleaf)

For the attention of Mrs D Smith

Dear Sirs
We acknowledge receipt of your recent letter...............

A name allows you to be more natural and direct:

Dear Mrs Smith

Thank you for...........

You will need a formal salutation when you write to an institution rather than a named reader.

A PLC or a limited company is a single legal entity and it is logical to address the company as Dear Sir. Avoid writing Dear Sir/Madam. Whichever part of that generalisation applies to it, it is offensive for its failure to relate properly to you. A general name can make a good alternative.

Use informative headings

Most letters will benefit from a heading. This serves to:

- tell the reader what you are writing about
- provides a descriptive reminder of the content of a letter you may later wish to retrieve.

In an extensive letter distinguish between a heading that covers the broad scope of the letter at the start:

Pullfir Contracts
Annual check J.Peters
Training programme

And the more specific headings that occur at intervals to identify the specific topics of the letter.

In a short letter you may write predominantly on one topic but then wish to make a small unrelated point later. This need produces clichés like:

May I take this opportunity to remind.............

While you are right to take the opportunity you will make a clear case by putting your thought under a separate heading. The letter will take on the following form:
Salutation
Heading one
....
....
....
Heading Two
....
Close

Think about the sequence in which you handle your headings. Where possible end with the topic that needs action.

Bullet points form a practical sub-structure for letters. They are best for items that require separate identification but which need no specific reference.

Before we can authorise a mortgage we will require:

- three payslips
- your P60
- proof of residence.

A sub-structure of numbers is helpful where you wish to raise a number of points which require a specific answer from your reader.

Start with the reasons for writing

Use the start of your letter to identify the reason for writing in the first place. When you initiate correspondence, spell out your intention for the reader. A heading will provide the initial view but your opening sequence will sharpen the focus:

- I am writing for information about the catering facilities that you offer.

- I plan to visit Sweden in the Summer

When responding to a letter you have a similar need to provide a clear focus for the reader. You may wish to use the heading from the original letter before responding more specifically:

- Thank you for your letter of 12th July.

- I confirm that our latest range of books will be ideal for your school.
- The plan enclosed with this letter should enable us to progress the matter.

Some very short letters end where they begin:

- Please send me a copy of your latest book and a catalogue
- I can confirm that I will be at the finance meeting next week

End by pointing the way ahead

The end of your letter is important in triggering the action you seek from the reader:
- Please let me know when you will send me my cheque.
- Please send me the completed form with payment by July 16th.

The true aim of the letter may vary from the issue that has prompted it. In such cases project your purpose at the end.

Long letters containing a number of action points may benefit from a short summary of actions at the end. Avoid clichés at the end of your letter. These usually appear when you have covered the ground and are ready to sign off. Padding at this point pushes the required action further back into the letter, making it less of a prompt for the reader's attention.

Matching the end of the letter to the salutation

There is a firm convention for matching the ending of a letter to the opening. If you begin with a proper noun:

Dear Mr Smith
Dear Miss Jones
You end:

Yours sincerely (the 's' is always lower case)
Similarly if you begin with a common noun:

Dear Leaseholder
Dear Lord Mayor

You end:

Yours sincerely

For formal salutations:

Dear Sir
Dear Madam

You end:

Yours faithfully
Composing Business letters

Writing effective letters is not just detailing information. The way you compose the letter, the format, is very important indeed. As well as the reader of the letter, you will need to consider:

- the sequence in which you deliver your letter
- the tone reflected in your choice of language.

Ask yourself, when putting the letter together:

- how firm should you be?
- should you be apologetic?
- Should you send enclosures?

And so on.

The sequence of a letter allows you to move:

- from where you are now
- by means of any supporting information
- to where you want to be.

Choosing an appropriate tone

When you write, your language conveys the content of the letter and the manner of its delivery. You should think very carefully about the words you use and the way you use them. Obviously, each letter is different and, in the context of business, there are many situations that you will need to address, from taking action against a member of staff, against a supplier, to praising someone for good work to chasing late payments.

79

One strand linking all letters is that of getting to the point as quickly as possible whilst getting the message across. The use of language is an art and a skill and it is very necessary to ensure that you have said all that you have to say, in a clear and (often) sensitive fashion. The aim is to get your message across and to convince or persuade the other of your case.

Summary and sample business letters.

In the last three chapters, several key points have been stressed. Before laying out sample business letters it is important to summarise these points:

- Aim your letter carefully. You should ask yourself why you are writing and who is your intended recipient. What does your reader need?

- Make sure you plan and structure your letter and decide the sequence of delivery. Take pains to ensure that your punctuation is correct and also control your sentence length.

Sample business letters

Overleaf.

Introducing your firm

PRINTING SERVICES LIMITED

Mr D Davies   38 King Road
Askews Castle Ltd   London E17 4PT
42 Smiths Drive
Aberdeen   Tel: 020 8123 5467
Perthshire
Scotland   Our ref:
321

21st July 20.....

Dear Mr Davies

I am writing to introduce my company to you. We care a business that provides printing services, consultancy and printing machinery to companies in the north of England. Our clients include Nobles, Bloomsbury and Polestar Wheaton Limited. In particular we offer:

- Cost effective printing solutions to meet all requirements.
- Consultancy services. These are designed to ascertain a clients needs.
- Follow up work with recommendations and costing.

At this stage, we enclose our latest brochure for your perusal. If you are interested in our products and services either now or in the future, please call me on my direct line 020 8123 5467. We would be pleased to supply further details on request or to discuss your requirements further.

Yours sincerely

David Askew
Sales manager

Offering new products

PRINTING SERVICES LIMITED

Mr D Davies   38 King Road
Askews Castle Ltd   London E17 9PT
42 Smiths Drive
Aberdeen   Tel: 020 8123 5467
Perthshire
Scotland

1st July 20......

Dear Mr Davies

We are pleased to introduce the latest addition to our fast expanding range of printing presses, the Digital plus reproduction unit. This innovative product is the latest in a line of presses introduced by Printing Services Limited. It is designed to enable small publishers to cut costs and keep their stock holdings down. There are tow distinctive features that distinguishes our press from others:

- Low print runs of 1 or more can be achieved.
- The press can achieve a two-week turnaround from placing of the order to fulfilment.

For a limited period, we are making a special offer available exclusively to our customers:

A 10% discount off the normal trade price for each press ordered.

We enclose sales literature for the press. To take advantage of this offer please ring me direct on 020 8123 5467. Please note that this offer is for a limited period. We look forward to receiving your call.
Yours sincerely

David Askew
Sales Manager

Chasing a reluctant buyer

PRINTING SERVICES LIMITED

Mr D Davies	38 King Road
Askews Castle Limited	London E17 9PT
42 Smith Drive	
Aberdeen	Tel: 020 8123 5467
Perthshire	
Scotland	Ref: 123

24th July 20......

Dear Mr Davies

We were delighted to receive your enquiry about our printing press last week. I understand that you expressed interest following a demonstration by our agent. We were sure that you would be impressed with the press and would appreciate the advantages to your company.

We can confirm that this product is still available at a 10% discount to you. However, we have to point out once again that this offer can extend for a limited period only as we have received many expressions of interests and resultant firm sales.

I am pleased to enclose our sales literature for your further perusal and information. Please do not hesitate to contact me to discuss the purchase of our press.
We look forward to hearing from you again.
Yours sincerely
David Askew

Sales manager
The three letters above demonstrate all of the key aims of a business letter. The letter is aimed at the key person, the message is clear. There is a clear understanding of what the reader needs. The letter is planned, structured and the sequence of delivery leaves the reader in no doubt as to the message.

The sentences are short, crisp and to the point. The reader will be very clear about the intent and will be impressed by the layout.

There are many varieties of business letters but the key themes are exactly the same throughout.

Now read the key points from Chapter 8

****

Key points from Chapter 8

- Letters have a certain convention that distinguishes them from e-mail and memoranda.

- Quote any references in full.

- Choose an appropriate salutation.

- Use informative headings.

- Start with the reasons for writing.

- End by pointing the way ahead.

- Choose an appropriate tone.

Ch. 9

Writing Personal Letters

So far, we have concentrated on the nature and form of business letters. These letters, by their nature, require a great deal of attention to detail as they act primarily as records of business and need to be specific in their aim.

Personal letters, whilst also ideally needing the same level of knowledge of the English language and attention to detail, have a different starting point. This is that they are personal and are often written to people we know and have conversed with many times. Therefore, many elements that we need to be aware of in business letters, such as the avoidance of jargon and clichés, are quite often present in personal letters.

Nevertheless, there are certain formal conventions that need to be observed at the outset.

Personal salutations

The personal letter will differ from the business letter in that you will usually put your name and address on the top right hand side, as with the example overleaf and the date under the address.

The letter will, in many cases, be handwritten, to add to the feeling of intimacy, and will finish not with 'Yours sincerely' but quite often will finish with 'love, or 'regards' or even 'cheers', depending on who you are writing to and how you have written the letter.

See example letter overleaf

Example personal letter.

> 38 Cromwell Road
> Walthamstow
> London E17 9JN

3rd May 20.....

Dear Peter

It was really great to see you at the opening match of the world cup last Wednesday. Hey, what a great game wasn't it? I really loved the first half and, although the second half dragged a bit there was loads of action.

Did you see Stanley Peters? What a real snake in the grass! He was excellent in the first half but was real lazy in the second. He should have been substituted.

Anyway, enough about football. What about you and your family? I hope that you are all faring well and Susan is OK. She is a really nice person and you have a very good partner there.

Well, old buddy, enough said. Once again, it was really great to see you and I look forward to the next time. We should get together a little earlier and maybe have a pint or two, just like old times. We wont overdo it, as we used to, but it would still be a nice break.

I am keeping well. Work is a bit of a bind but there again, isn't all work nowadays. Very stressy. Take care mate, see you soon I hope.

Cheers
Dave

As you can see, this letter is full of the elements that have been advised against in a business letter. This is precisely because personal letters are personal and you are often talking to people with whom you have built up a relationship over the years. You know and understand the person and the type of language that is acceptable, therefore the use of clichés, jargon and so on is perfectly acceptable.

In many ways, the personal letter is the opposite of the business letter in that, in the business letter, you are trying to portray a positive image, well constructed and to the point with the express aim of communicating your message in a formal way.

You would certainly never handwrite a business letter, or finish by saying 'cheers'.

In some cases, with a personal letter, you may wish to adopt a mix of formal and personal. If you were writing to your Uncle Tom, who you have not seen for twenty years, you would not be writing in a very chummy style and yet you would not be over-personal either. You would use some elements of intimacy connected with the family and family memories but you would also be looking to present a rather formal image as you do not know this person well enough to adopt a chummy approach.

The art and craft of writing personal letters very much depends on you as a person, the person you are communicating to and also what you are trying to say. If you are in correspondence with a friend or acquaintance who is interested in politics and you are discussing political events then you would probably need to be well versed in the language and grammar, as well as current affairs, to be able to express yourself effectively.

If you are discussing matters of the heart then you would need to be possessed of a language and style that allowed you to express yourself sensitively. In many cases, the advantage of knowing the English language, and the ability to express your self, bringing into play all the elements of language, such as grammar and punctuation, will prove to be a great asset. It is hoped that the brief introduction contained within this book will assist that process.

Now read the key points from Chapter 9 overleaf.

****

Key points from Chapter 9

- Personal letters have a different starting point to business letters.

- Although personal letters are less formal than business letters, there are still formal conventions to be followed.

- The personal letter will differ to the business letter in that the writer will normally put their name and address on the right hand side.

- The letter will finish with a variety of different endings depending who you are writing to.

Ch. 10

Editing and Proofreading

Editing and proofreading letters is perhaps one of the most important elements in the production of effective letters, whether business or personal.

An effective editor/proof reader will need a range of skills, including a sound knowledge of the English language and of the intricacies of grammar. This book has, hopefully, allowed the reader to absorb the basic structure of the language.

You should always allow time for proof reading and understand that the task is part of the process of producing a letter.

Focussing on proof reading

Many environments are not ideal for proofreading so you should try to find a space where you can work comfortably without interruption. If your letter is complex or technical you may prefer to enlist some help to read the 'dead' copy (first draft) while you concentrate on producing the live (original) copy. Proof reading is about detail. However, we need to be aware of the broader impression of the piece of writing. You should proof read for:
- visual impression
- sense of the message
- accuracy of the detail.

Visual impression

What does the page look like? Is there too much detail on the page and is there enough white space? Is the page balanced between top and bottom and if there is a large gap at the bottom is this intended? Is the text justified? Is it aligned to the left only? Are headings too large or small and is the size of typeface appropriate?

Reading for sense

This aspect can test your knowledge of grammar and ability to write clearly.

Are the paragraph breaks in the right place and are sentences too long? Is there enough variety in the sentence structure? Are there errors of grammar and is the word order correct? Is the message of the letter clear?

Reading for detail

You should expect to find errors at the start of the text and near other errors. In addition, errors will appear in common words which are usually mixed up, such as:

- not/no
- there/the
- and/an

Errors will also appear when repeating from the end of a line to the beginning of the next line, in changes from standard type and in changes of page formation: margins, columns etc.

It is easy to rationalise these errors. Changes of type or page formation cause us to think about control instructions rather than the flow of typing. Some word processing software will not show the end of one line and the beginning of the next line simultaneously on the monitor.

You will be reassured by the relative ease with which you will find errors such as omitted letters, spaces, punctuation marks or substitutions of one letter for another. You will also be aware of the need to concentrate carefully when you proof read a letter properly You should ensure that you proof read a letter twice to ensure that you have not missed mistakes.

Check you are clear and concise

No single aspect of your writing will produce a clear, conciso style: you will need to review a number of elements.

Sequence
- check that your letter achieves a progression of ideas
- see that you move from where you are at the start to where you want to be at the end.

Paragraphs

A paragraph that might suit a long report can look excessive when applied to another letter:

- make paragraphs in letters relatively short
- make the topic of each paragraph clear

- if you have divided a paragraph, see that the new paragraph has a clear headline and is not left dangling by a pronoun.

Sentences

- check your sentence length
- aim for an average of twenty words but vary your sentence length for interest.
- Remember that a series of short sentences can read like a menu.

Punctuation

- see that punctuation properly supports the structure of your writing.
- Be sure the reader will absorb the meaning in a single reading.
- If the punctuation is struggling to reveal your meaning rewrite the sentence

Active voice

- link subject and verb directly by presenting your case in the active voice.

Familiar words

- use familiar words that will be comfortable for the reader

Concrete words

- use concrete words to paint a clear picture for the reader.
- Make your specification explicit and complete

Cliches

- avoid over used business expressions
- use your own words to set the right tone and help a flow of ideas.

Jargon

- Use jargon to tune in to the reader
- Avoid jargon that will sound out of tune.

Fulfil your aim

Ask yourself key questions:

- who will read my letter?
- What does my reader need to know?
- What did I need to know?
- Is the required action clear?
- Will the reader know when to respond?

Proof reading and editing is an important skill and it is essential that letters are read and amended as necessary. Treat your first letter as a first draft that will need fine-tuning before you send it.

If you are writing a particularly emotive letter, sometimes it is better to sleep on it for a night rather than send it immediately.

Now read the key points from chapter 10 overleaf.

****

Key points from Chapter 10

- Editing and proofreading is one of the most important elements when writing a letter, particularly a business letter.

- An effective proof-reader will need a range of skills, including a sound knowledge of the English language.

- Proof reading is about detail.

- In addition to detail you should be aware of the broader impression of a piece of writing, such as visual impression, sense of message and accuracy of detail.

Ch. 11

Writing Effective emails

In the previous chapters, we have covered business and personal letters. In this chapter we will cover business emails and also e mails that cover job applications and also marketing emails.

Business emails

In many cases now, whereas once upon a time a letter was necessary to confirm a deal or to agree on a business deal, now it is quite common to use an e mail. Because email is a rather different form of correspondence then it follows that there are slightly different rules to follow.

Although emails are often seen as less formal than printed business letters, in the business world you cannot afford to let your language appear to be informal. Email may be faster and more efficient, but your client or business partner will not easily forgive correspondence that is too casual.

Begin with a greeting

It's important to always open your email with a greeting, such as "Dear Peter,". Depending on the formality of your relationship, you may want to use their family name as opposed to their given name, i.e. "Dear Mrs. Davies,". If the relationship is more casual, you can simply say, "Hi Susan," If you're contacting a company, not an individual, you may write "To Whom It May Concern:" Thank the recipient If you are replying to a client's inquiry, you should begin with a line of thanks. For example, if someone has a question about your company, you can say, "Thank you for contacting (XXX) Company."

If someone has replied to one of your emails, be sure to say, "Thank you for your prompt reply." or "Thanks for getting back to me." If you can find any way to thank the reader, then do. It will put him or her at ease, and it will make you appear more courteous.

State your purpose

If, however, you are initiating the email communication, it may be impossible to include a line of thanks. Instead, begin by stating your purpose. For example, "I am writing to enquire about ..." or "I am writing in reference to ..." It's important to make your purpose clear early on in the email, and then move into the main text of your email.

Good Grammar!

Remember to pay careful attention to grammar, spelling and punctuation, and to avoid run-on sentences by keeping your sentences short and clear.

Closing remarks

Before you end your email, it's polite to thank your reader one more time as well as add some courteous closing remarks. You might start with "Thank you for your patience and cooperation." or "Thank you for your consideration." and then follow up with, "If you have any questions or concerns, don't hesitate to let me know." and "I look forward to hearing from you." End with a closing The last step is to include an appropriate closing with your name. "Best regards," "Sincerely," and "Thank you," are all professional. It's a good idea to avoid closings such as "Best wishes," or "Cheers," as these are best used in casual, personal emails. Finally, before you hit the send button, review and spell check your email one more time to make sure it's truly perfect! -

The following are some tips to help you when you are writing business letters through email.

- o A heading is not necessary in an email (your return address, their address, and the date).
- o Use a descriptive subject line.
- o Avoid using an inappropriate or silly email address; register a professional sounding address if you don't have one.
- o Use simple formatting, keep everything flush with the left margin; avoid special formatting and tabs.
- o Keep your letter formal, just because it's an email instead of a hard copy is no excuse for informality (don't forget to use spell check and proper grammar).

o   Try to keep your letter less than 80 characters wide, some email readers will create line breaks on anything longer and ruin the formatting.
o   If possible, avoid attachments unless the recipient has requested or is expecting an attachment. If it is a text document, simply cut and paste the text below your letter and strip out any special formatting.
o   If the person's name is unknown, address the person's title e.g. Dear Director of Human Resources.

Job application emails

As with business emails, it is now common to email companies with CV's, job applications and cover letters. Your covering email is quite important as this is quite often the first thing that a prospective employer might see. First impressions can be lasting impressions!

Subject line

After you have checked that you have the right email address, you need to make sure that you put the right information in the subject line. This immediately shows the respondent what the email is about and ensures that it does not get overlooked or counted as spam.

Addressing the email

In the same way as a covering letter, a covering email should be addressed to the right person as outline don the job specification.

Be sure to address the recipient in the correct manner, either as 'Mr' or 'Mrs' or 'Ms' (if you are not sure of status). If the job specification simply states 'S. Wilson' then just address sit S Wilson as guessing can be quite insulting if you get it wrong.

If you are applying for a job that requires an initial covering letter then it is a good idea to keep your email short and to the point. One paragraph is enough which should act as an introduction to you as a person, what you can bring to the company in question and why you are applying for the position.

Attachments

If you need to attach your CV and covering letter to your email, there are a few things that you need to be wary about. Firstly, make sure that your documents are named correctly.-simply calling your CV 'CV' isn't very descriptive, especially when your potential employer is likely to be drowning in them. make sure you include your name when naming your documents and be sure to actually attach them to your email before sending. Its surprising how many people forget!

When signing off your email, you should try to end with something positive and polite like; "Thank you for taking the time to review my application. I look forward to hearing from you". This will show that you are enthusiastic and polite, two attributes that all employers want to see.

Also be sure to sign off with "Kind Regards" or "Yours Sincerely" rather than something chatty or informal.

Taking time over your email should help you in your quest for a job. First impressions, lasting impressions!

Email marketing

According to some estimates, more than 144 billion emails are sent every day—and, sometimes, it seems like every one of them lands in your inbox. We all know what it's like to be bombarded with email messages—all competing for a share of our attention during a busy day.

There are certain rules to adopt when using emails for the purpose of marketing. As we all know, marketing emails can seem annoying and irrelevant. We delete them more often than not. There is also the problem of spam and what it might do to your computer. Below are a few tips to help you construct an effective marketing e mail which might get read.

Email marketing

If it's your job to come up with a subject line that is compelling enough to cut through all that clutter, it's a good idea to apply your experience as an email recipient to help you craft the perfect subject line. What gets your attention? How do you decide which emails to trash unopened and which to read? Scores of scientific studies can tell you which words appear with the most frequency in successful email campaigns. And that is useful information. But in creating a compelling subject line, sometimes a simple strategy works best.

Keep it brief

When prospects are scanning their inboxes, a short, snappy subject is more likely to catch their eye than a lengthier line. If possible, it's best to keep the subject line short enough to appear as one line on a smaller device screen, such as a smartphone or tablet. Keep it short and sweet to improve your open and rates.

Don't waste valuable space

A subject line doesn't provide much space, so make every word count. Don't waste space with words (such as "hello") that don't add much value to your message. When crafting your subject line, evaluate each word and make sure it adds value—from the standpoint of providing information or encouraging readers to open the email.

Be specific

When readers are scanning new messages in their inbox, they're generally in a hurry to respond to urgent messages or tackle the next task in their busy day. In such a state of mind, they won't have much patience for mystery. Cut to the chase by using the subject line to tell them what the message is about.

Make it searchable

There's a good chance your reader won't have time to focus on your message when they first see it, so it's wise to give them an easy way to return to the message when they have more time. If you make the subject line searchable so readers can easily find it later, there's a better chance that they'll revisit your email, even if they don't have time at first.

Include a call to action

Make sure your subject line tells the reader what he or she can do to benefit from the message—whether that's to visit a site, make a call, or just read the message. A brief line that summarizes the value can be highly effective, so think about what's in it for the reader and try to convey that in the subject line.

Don't create anxiety

Although you want your readers to take action, it's important to balance a call to action with a signal that you respect their time. Subject lines that include phrases such as "immediate response required" can come across as arrogant. Adding "FYI" or "no need to reply" can take the pressure off while still signalling that the message contains valuable information.

Include your company name

Readers will be more likely to open an email if they know who it's from and if they perceive value from the sending organization. Including a company name is especially important if you already have a positive relationship with the reader.

Email is one of the major ways how we communicate in business. The issue isn't email itself, but inbox overload and finding a way to separate the mundane and annoying from the truly important.

There are proven ways to tame overflowing inboxes, and every professional needs a sound strategy. Your challenge as an email marketer is to ensure that your message makes the cut.

****

Glossary of terms

Acronym. A word formed from the initial letters of other words.

Adjective. A word that describes a noun.

Adverb. A word that qualifies a verb, an adjective or other adverb.

Clause, dependent. A main group of words containing a verb that depends on the main clause. They cannot stand alone.

Conjunction. A word that links two main clauses together.

Gerund. A present participle used as a noun.

Inverted commas. Speech marks put around speech and quotations.

Jargon. Words or expressions used by a certain group of people.

Justify. Adjust margins so that they are level.

Metaphor. An implied comparison of two things.

Noun, abstract. A word that denotes a quality or state.

Noun, collective. A singular word which refers to a group of people or things.

113

Noun, common. The name of a thing.

Noun, proper. The name of a person or place. It always begins with a capital letter.

Object. A noun or pronoun that follows the verb and is related to the subject.

Paragraph. A group of sentences dealing with the same topic.

Personify. Giving a humane object human characteristics.

Phrase. A group of words not necessarily containing a verb or making sense on its own.

Preposition. A word that governs a noun or pronoun.

Pronoun, interrogative. A pronoun that is used at the start of a question.

Pronoun, personal. A word that takes the place of a noun.

Pronoun, relative. This has a similar role to a conjunction. It joins clauses together but is closely linked to a noun.

Simile. A comparison of two things using 'like' or 'as'.

Subject. The noun or pronoun on which the rest of the clause depends.

Synonym. A word that can be used to replace another.

Tautology. A statement that is repeated in a different way in the same sentence.

Thesaurus. A book which will give a collection of synonyms.

****

Straightforward Guides If you would like to know more about Straightforward Guides email us at:

info@straightforwardco.co.uk or please write to:

59 Abingdon Street Derby DE24 8GA.

Index

Exclamation marks, 20

F
Familiar words, 8, 99
Finite verbs, 24
Forming paragraph structure, 7, 65
Forming plurals, 5, 32
Forming words, 5, 31
Full stop, 68
Full stops, 16

G
Gerund, 113

H
Handling contractions, 6, 40
Headings, 74

J
Jargon, 9, 48, 99, 113
Justify, 113

L
Layout of Letters, 71
Long vowels, 33

M
Metaphors, 49

N
Non-finite verbs, 24

Noun, 113, 114

****

www.straightforwardco.co.uk

All titles, listed below, in the Straightforward Guides Series can be purchased online, using credit card or other forms of payment by going to www.straightfowardco.co.uk A discount of 25% per title is offered with online purchases.

Law

A Straightforward Guide to:

Consumer Rights
Bankruptcy Insolvency and the Law
Employment Law
Private Tenants Rights
Family law
Small Claims In the County Court
Contract law
Intellectual Property and the law
Divorce and the law
Leaseholders Rights
The Process of Conveyancing
Knowing Your Rights and Using the Courts
Producing Your own Will
Housing Rights
The Bailiff the law and You
Probate and The Law
Company law
What to Expect When You Go to Court
Guide to Competition Law
Give me Your Money-Guide to Effective Debt Collection

Caring for a Disabled Child

General titles

Letting Property for Profit
Buying, Selling and Renting property
Buying a Home in England and France
Bookkeeping and Accounts for Small Business
Creative Writing
Freelance Writing
Writing Your own Life Story
Writing performance Poetry
Writing Romantic Fiction
Speech Writing
Teaching Your Child to Read and write
Teaching Your Child to Swim
Raising a Child-The Early Years
Creating a Successful Commercial Website
The Straightforward Business Plan
The Straightforward C.V.
Successful Public Speaking
Handling Bereavement
Play the Game-A Compendium of Rules
Individual and Personal Finance
Understanding Mental Illness
The Two Minute Message
Guide to Self Defence
Tiling for Beginners

Go to: www.straightforwardco.co.uk